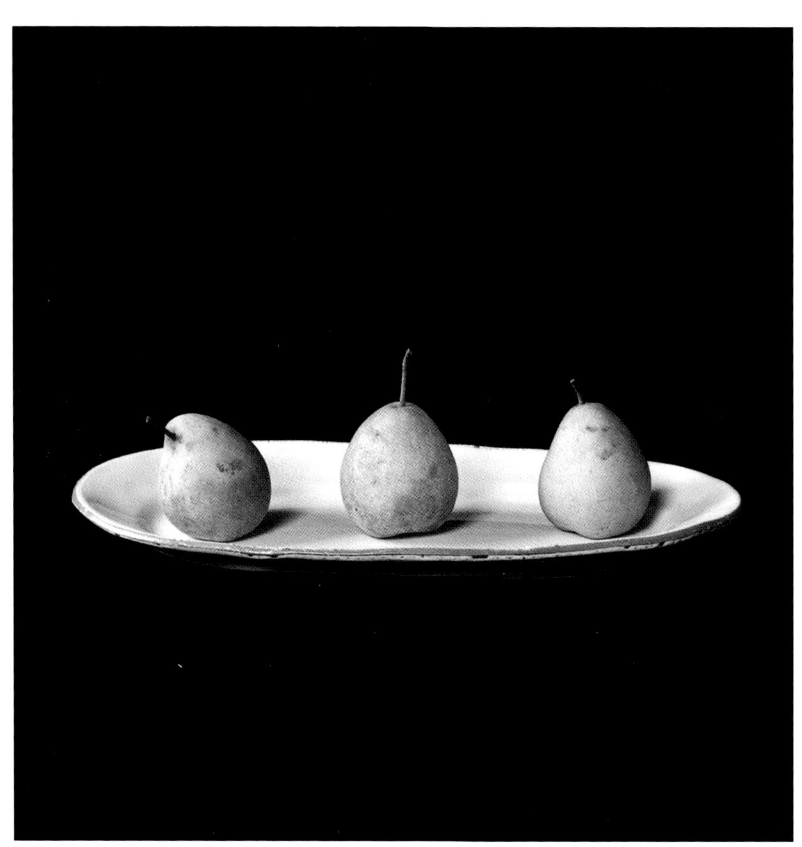

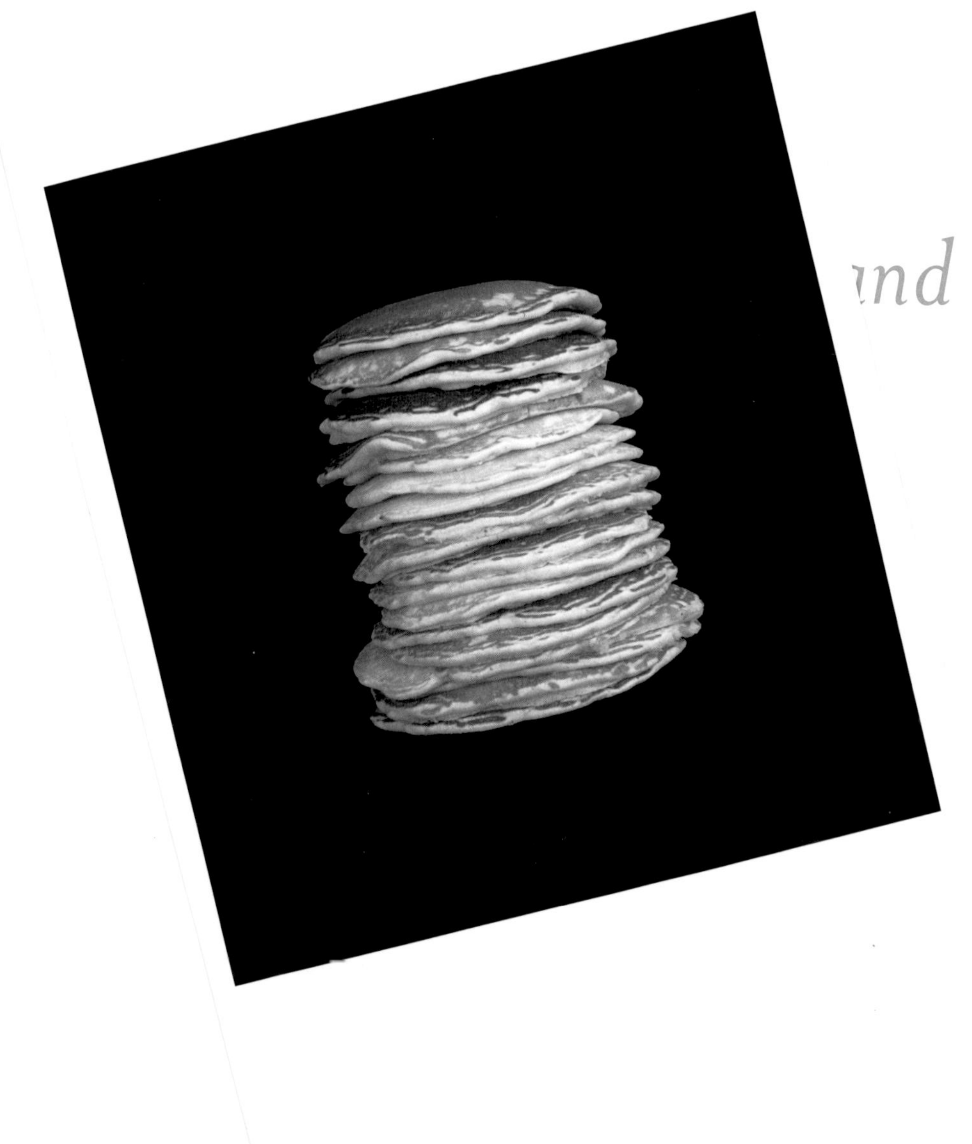

The Quantuck Lane Press
New York

Printed in Italy

First Edition

Composition and book design by Debbie Berne,
Herter Studio LLC, San Francisco

Manufacturing by Mondadori Printing, Verona

Library of Congress Cataloging-in-Publication Data

Cook, Mariana Ruth.
Close at hand / Mariana Cook ; introduction by
Arthur Sze. — 1st ed.
p. cm.
ISBN 978-1-59372-032-2
1. Photography, Artistic. 2. Cook, Mariana Ruth.
I. Title.
TR655.C66 2007
779.092--dc22
2007010048

The Quantuck Lane Press
New York
www.quantucklanepress.com

Distributed by: W.W. Norton & Company,
500 Fifth Avenue, New York, NY 10110
www.wwnorton.com

W.W. Norton & Company Ltd., Castle House,
75/76 Wells Street, London, WIT 3QT

1 2 3 4 5 6 7 8 9 0

for Emily and Hans

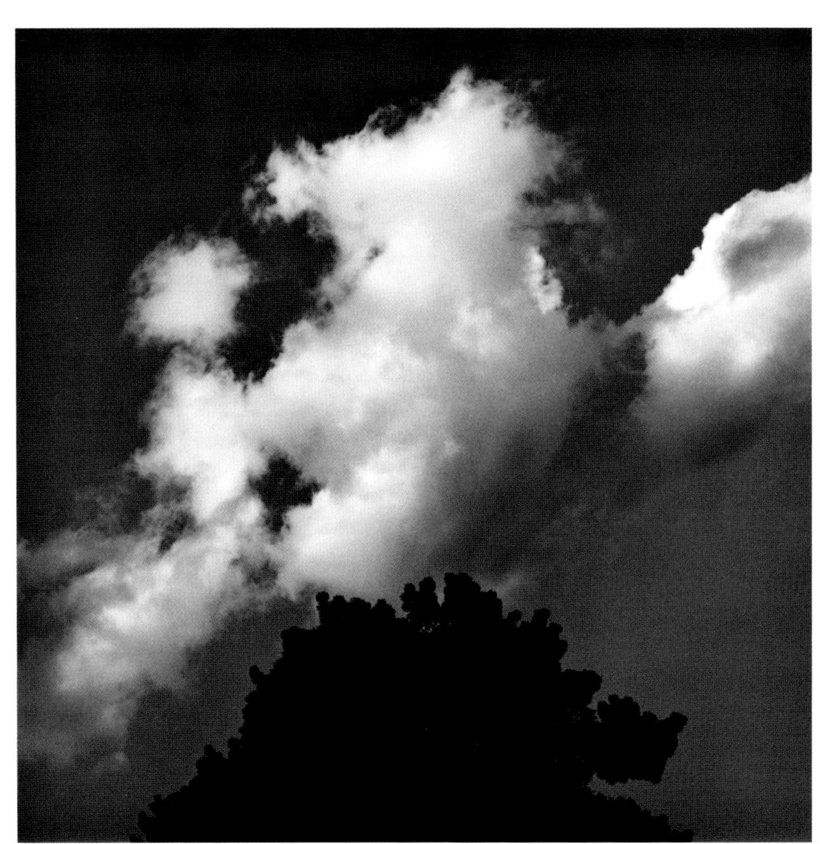

To see a world in a grain of sand,
And a heaven in a wild flower,
Hold infinity in the palm of your hand,
And eternity in an hour....

William Blake
Augeries of Innocence

*I*ntroduction

by Arthur Sze

HAZELNUTS, A DOORKNOB, cherry tree in blossom, platane tree bark, pool steps under water, eggplant, pussy willows, roof, a blind chicken, white peach, shadow of hand, light, Cubanelle pepper, clouds, door jamb, yo-yos, jellyfish, stonemason's bucket, chayote, sand, sourdough boule, three pears on a plate, child's torso, shaded window handles, hydrangea in a vase, water reflection, construction tarp, hat—these are some of the splendors in this new book by Mariana Cook.

For those familiar with Mariana Cook's previous work in portraiture—*Fathers and Daughters, Mothers and Sons, Generations of Women, Couples, Faces of Science*—this new volume is a bold and exciting development.

Starting on January 1, 1999 and continuing through the next eight years, Mariana Cook took a photograph a day. As simple as that. Wherever she was: New York City; Chilmark; Basel; Rome; Santa Barbara; Kent, Connecticut—wherever. And at whatever time: 4:40, 10:30, 9:45, 6:10, 4:50, 8:25—whenever she chose.

You might initially think of these photographs as a diary or log, but that idea quickly proves inadequate. There is no confessing here, nor is there a story that builds in intensity toward a climax. Yet intensity is clearly here. And passion, rhythm, rigor, and beauty. These photographs burn in the retina and then in the body and mind. They unfold with uncanny and luminous elegance, yet there is no formal closure: they remain open to darkness and to the intensity of seeing, minute by minute, day by day. Indeed, Mariana Cook's photographs disorient and startle us in order to accomplish their more enduring effects.

You can trace the inner rhythm of this book by tracking the images of trees. First, there are clouds and tree in West Tisbury, Massachusetts, then an oak tree, treetops and clouds, a Chilmark oak, three birch trees, cherry tree in blossom, Central Park trees, tree trunk in sky.

In "Oak Tree," you see the rhythmical pulse and twist of branches; there are no leaves to obscure the view. Here the life force is sinuous and shocking in its vigor; you rarely see it so exposed.

Sometimes in looking up, it is as if you are looking down, deeply, into the nature of things. In "Cherry Tree in Blossom," you look up at the branches that arc, undulate and thin to the very twig. The white blossoms, in clusters, fan out so that there are erratic glimpses, or episodes, of sky. In looking up at the branches and blossoms, everything is interconnected, in ways you couldn't anticipate. But you can see it now, and the world is in bloom.

As in music, there are returns, or variations on a theme, which you can find by juxtaposing various photographs. Consider "Hazelnuts" next to "Clouds, Lambert's Cove," where high, fluffy clouds and the spaces between them fill the frame. Appearance and reality, or, rather, apparition and actuality are haunting polarities here.

I like to think of "Hazelnuts" as a cornerstone of this book. You can stare at them and revel in their shapes. Some have slight cracks; some are whole; almost all are streaked. Each one is distinct, and the cumulative effect is to see hazelnuts as you have never seen them before. They are many, and yet together they are one. When I look again, I begin to focus on the dark spaces between the hazelnuts; it's what I can't see that begins to haunt.

Indeed, Mariana Cook's photographs lend themselves to meditation and incantation. Here are further musings on personal favorites: "Pool": two irregular lines of irregular dark tiles slant from the lower right to the upper left; the rest of the bottom of the pool is formed by light-colored tiles, or stones. Or so it seems. The water on the surface appears to be rippling. In motion. Waves. It's slightly dizzying when you try to look to the bottom; there is always a transparent interference, shimmer, ache.

"Bosc pear": is this pear upright with a black background or viewed from above? What could be simpler and yet more passionate? Look at the sensuous shape, heft, and mottled skin: it has an irregular weight at the bottom then tapers upward, flaring into its fibrous twists in the stem. Each small thing in the world has its own signature yet creates a tiny shock wave with its form and weight. You rarely notice an object with such clarity, but here you experience it with enormous immediacy.

"Pantheon": think of a lens or a tunnel or astronomical turning of light. At first, it is as if you are looking up into the highest part of a dome and out into the sky; there's the curvature of space, and time. And then it's about turning and being turned. Who is looking and from where? Where, or what, is the aperture of light? Does one always have to look up? Or, in a shift of perception, is it a smooth porcelain disk on a black sheet?

"Pussy Willows": does darkness precede light? Against a deep black background, it is amazing that there is anything at all; yet pussy willows arc up from the bottom and flare out across the space. Their irregular shapes and buds are the arabesque of spring: frail, delicate, incipient. And they are celebrated with a warm, loving eye.

"Self-Portrait": in a rare moment, you see the photographer in the lower left quadrangle with camera, tripod, wristwatch, unflinching gaze. What are in the other quadrants with such varied textures? Is it a pressed or linen screen that catches the light in different ways? Are there one or two or three screens? Because the focus of attention is primarily on objects, it is appropriate the photographer is off-center, down to the left, staring toward a trapezoidal-shaped area of light, and for the multiple dividers to form quadrants, the mysterious textures and uncharted maps of experience.

I could go on, but I want to return to the original splendor of the photographs. The uncompromising eye. The rigor. The elegance. And in the close attention to detail, warmth and passion.

Mariana Cook's photographs make us consider actuality and apparition, being and becoming: the great stillness and motions of the world. By making us focus and see with clarity and intensity, her photographs give us a renewed sense of the miraculous. And where we may yearn for what appears to be far away, it is wonderful to realize that the miraculous is in fact, indeed, always, "Close at hand."

Artist's Statement

I NEED TO WORK CREATIVELY, to sublimate energy which might otherwise be self-destructive into something searching, hopeful, and tangible. After completing four large bodies of portrait work, I didn't know what to do next. The thought of not working terrified me. Once it became clear that I wouldn't be able to settle on a theme, a solution presented itself. I would simply make one photograph a day for a year, the last year of the twentieth century. Each day's subject could be whatever I chose.

I began the project on the first of January 1999. The world at large was thinking about time—the end of one millennium and the beginning of another. It is somehow fitting, though not calculated, that the subject of the first picture in the series is of light emerging from darkness. Light—elusive, uncontrollable—is first and foremost what inspires me to make photographs. It was not the first time light itself had been the subject of one of my photographs, but here it served as my first step into and perhaps out of the unknown. I'd planned to make a picture a day for a year. The year turned into three and while the daily routine has relaxed since then, I continue to make pictures in the same vein.

I claim no novelty for the exercise. Early in 1999, I met a friend who told me he was writing one poem a day for the year, and we were both excited about our new endeavors. But when I saw my friend again six months later, he told me he had abandoned the project because he learned that someone else had already written one poem a day for a year. Well yes, but were they the same poems? It was the daily rhythm that I had committed to, not the product that kept me going. My photographs, some disappointing and some unexpectedly good, came into being only because I had pledged myself to keep at it.

A few people have suggested that all the pictures I made in 1999 should be reproduced here. They believe that documenting the work in its entirety was the point of the project. That's not how I see it. For me the process matters because of the results it yields. The daily aspect is only meaningful because pictures exist which wouldn't otherwise.

In 2000, I saw an exhibit of photographs which were taken by a photographer every day for many, many years. The work was expressive in "a life of the everyday man" way and yet the sequence lacked dramatic narrative, tension, development; the effects you achieve only by the pressure of selection.

I have always felt at a certain remove from the wider world, from popular culture, from the press of public events. I fear crowds—subways, streets, carnivals, places abuzz with activity. Making one photograph a day, given my circumscribed habits then, forced me to look anew at my home, nearby surroundings and habitual travels. I saw my daughter's feet in the sand, an egg, the French tulips my husband gave me for my birthday, the pancakes a friend made for brunch in our home. As time went on, I found myself gravitating toward abstraction and transformation: The forms contained within the object. Fruit and vegetables, flowers, a tree, shadows—suddenly these things registered on my consciousness and the familiar became strange. The work has no relation to time and it calls spatial definition into question.

Hidden in plain view, the ordinary things around me—overlooked for years—proved to harbor worlds of their own by turn simple and surreal. What began as a straightforward effort to secure myself, day after day, became unnerving and sometimes frightening. It has left me with these images, and with a question. Where do I turn now?

Mariana Cook

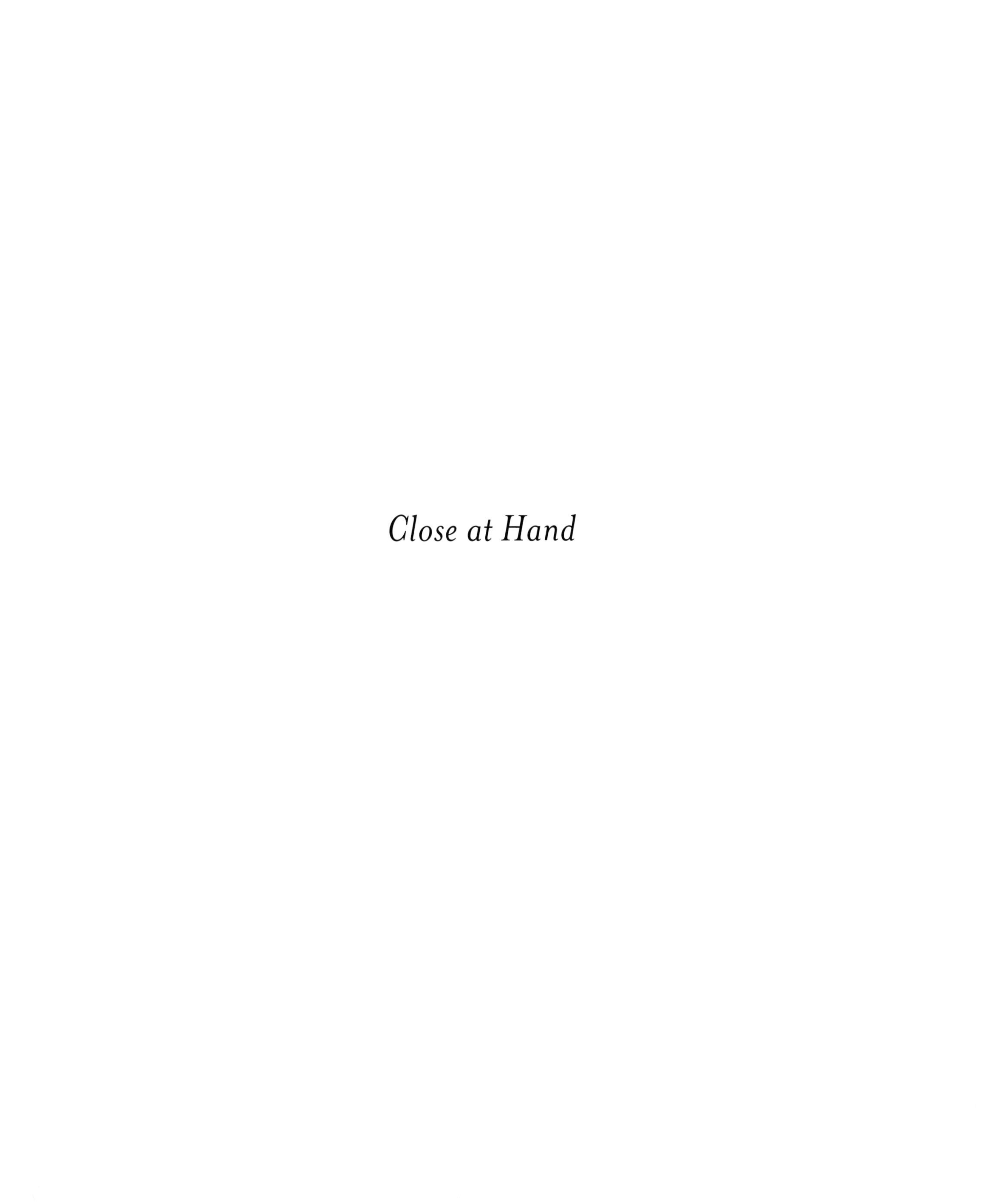

Close at Hand

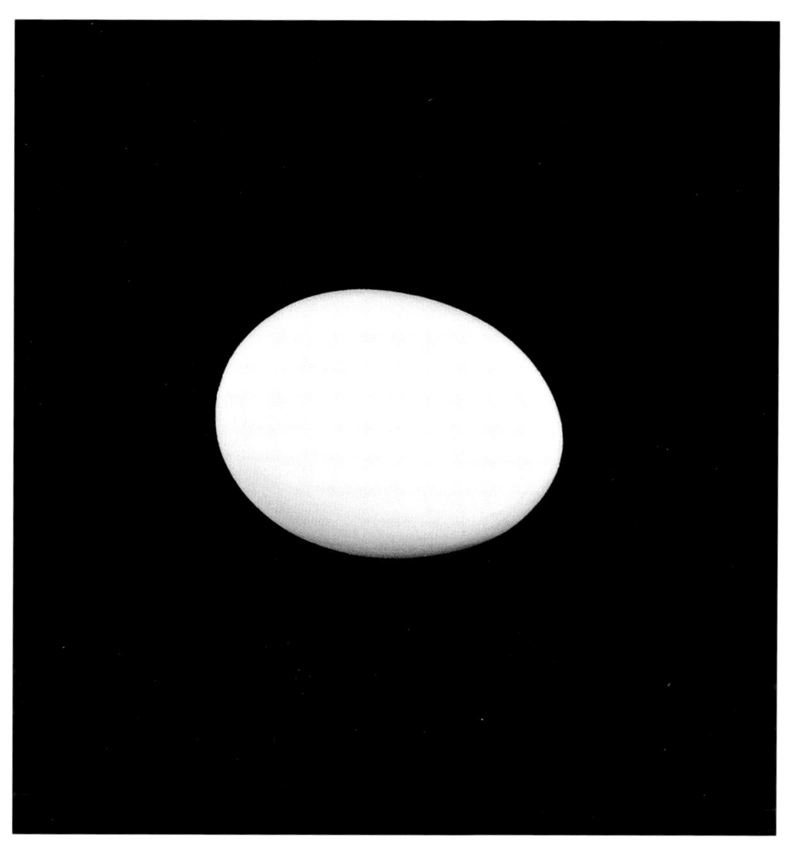

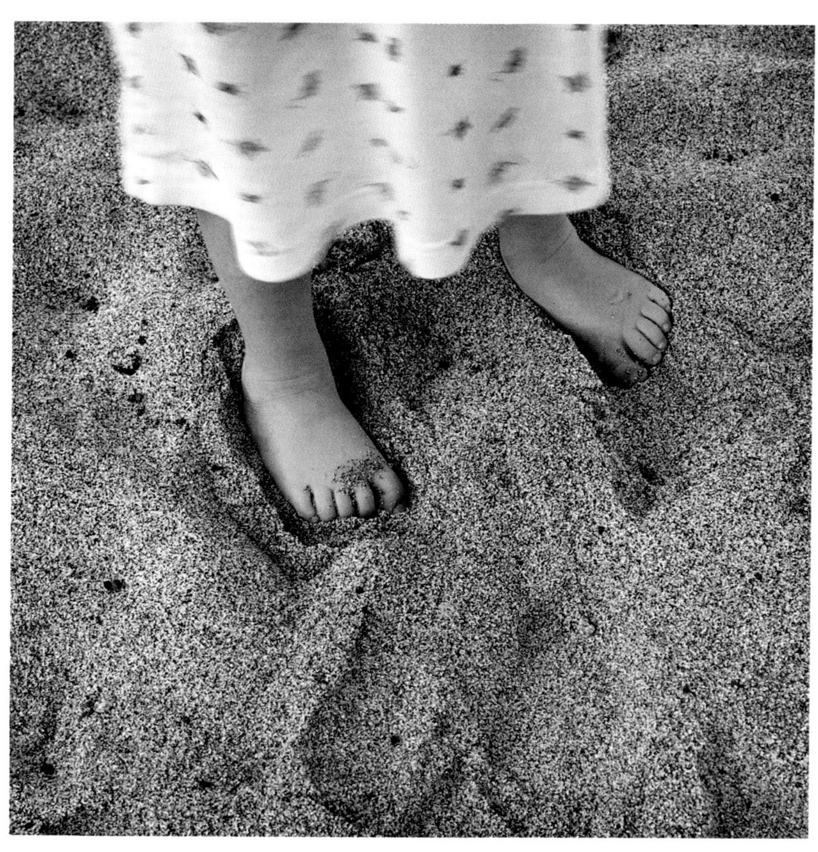

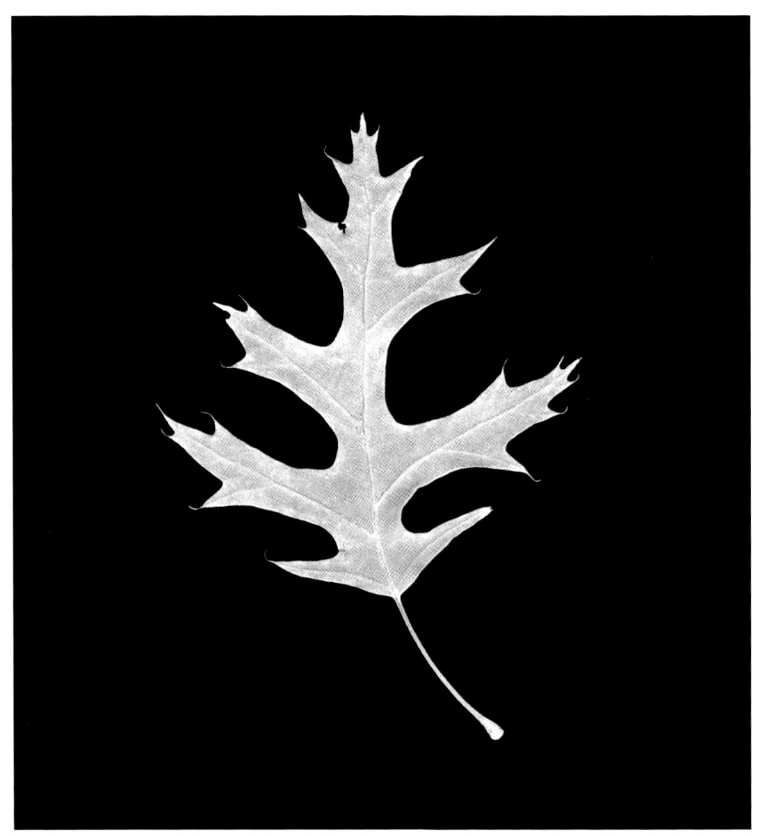

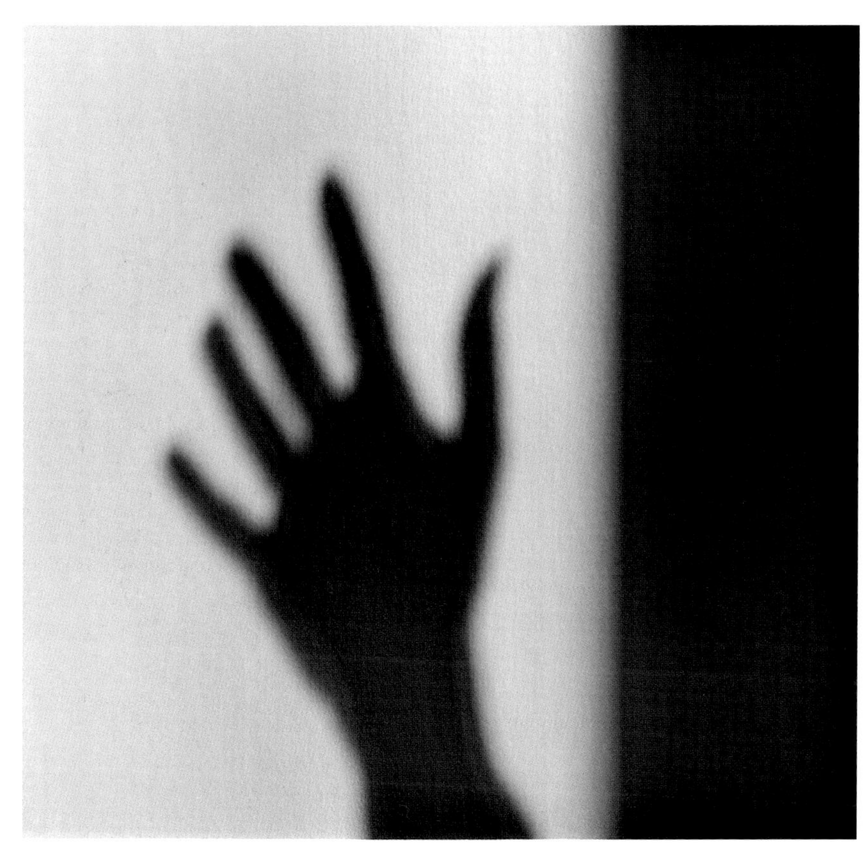

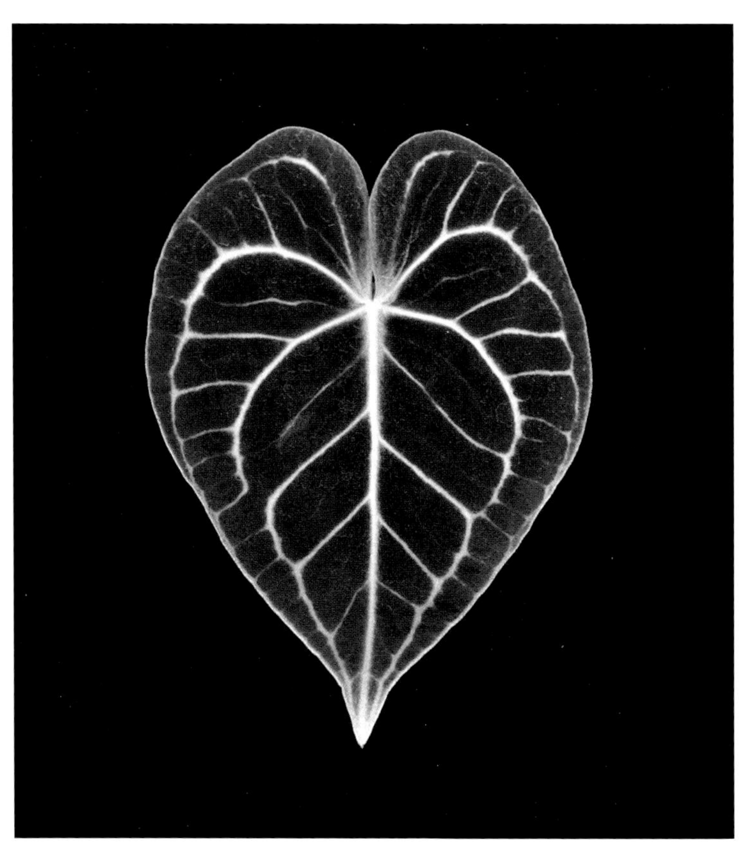

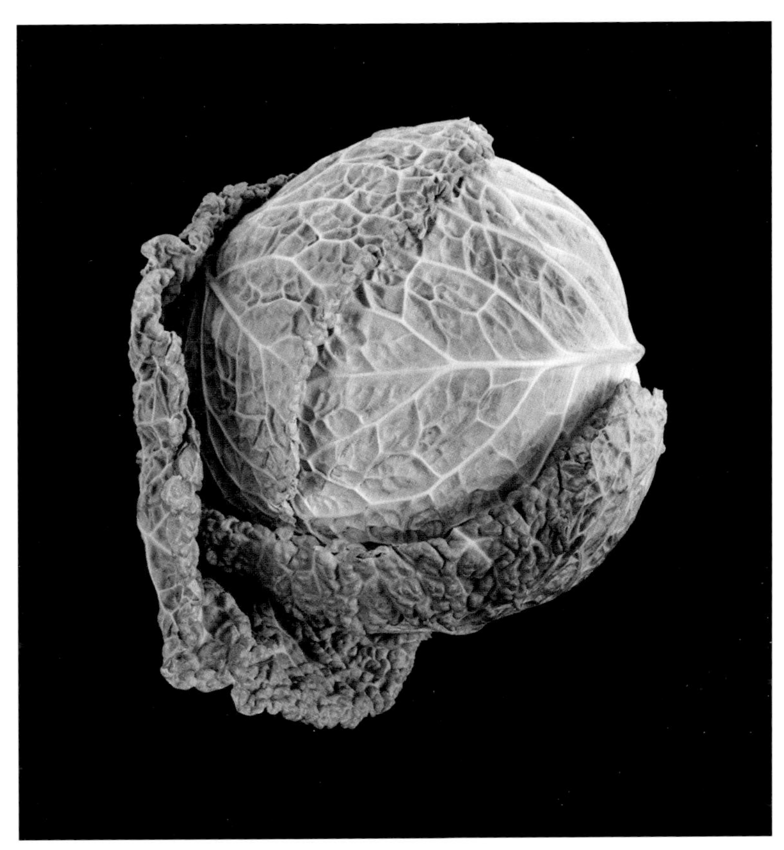

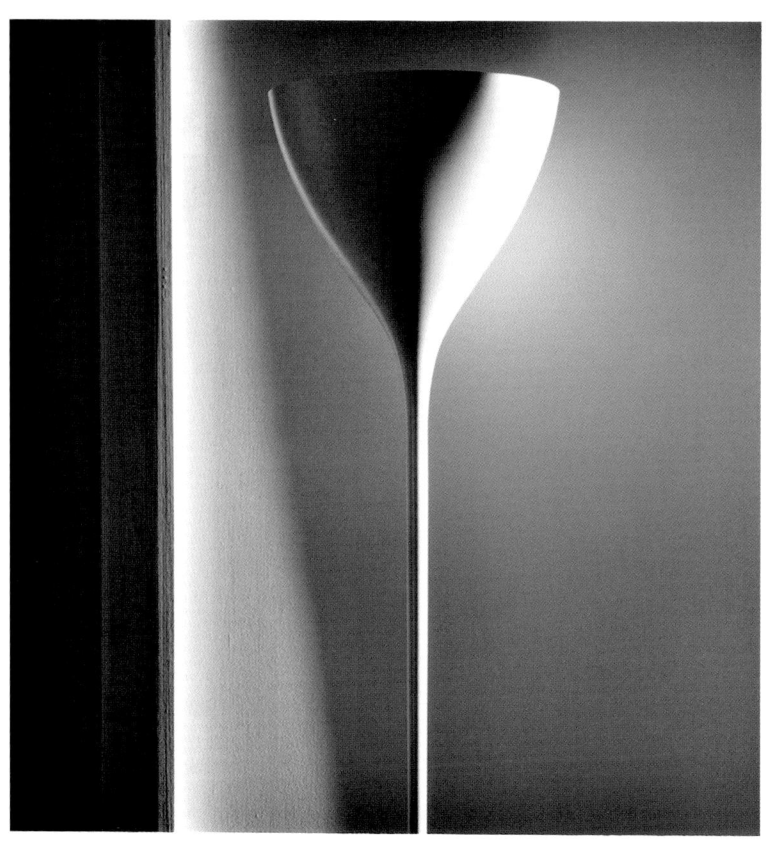

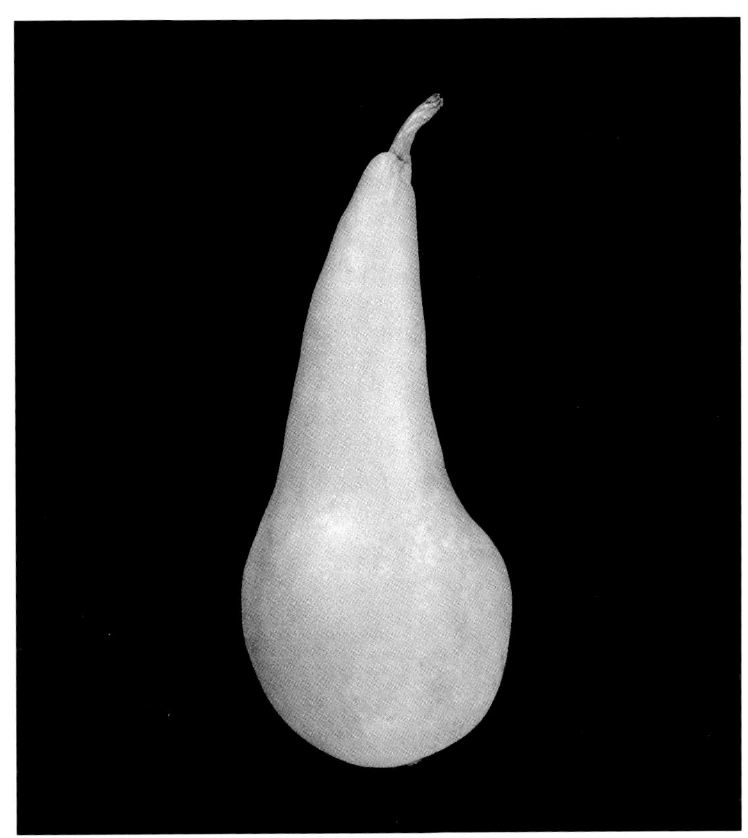

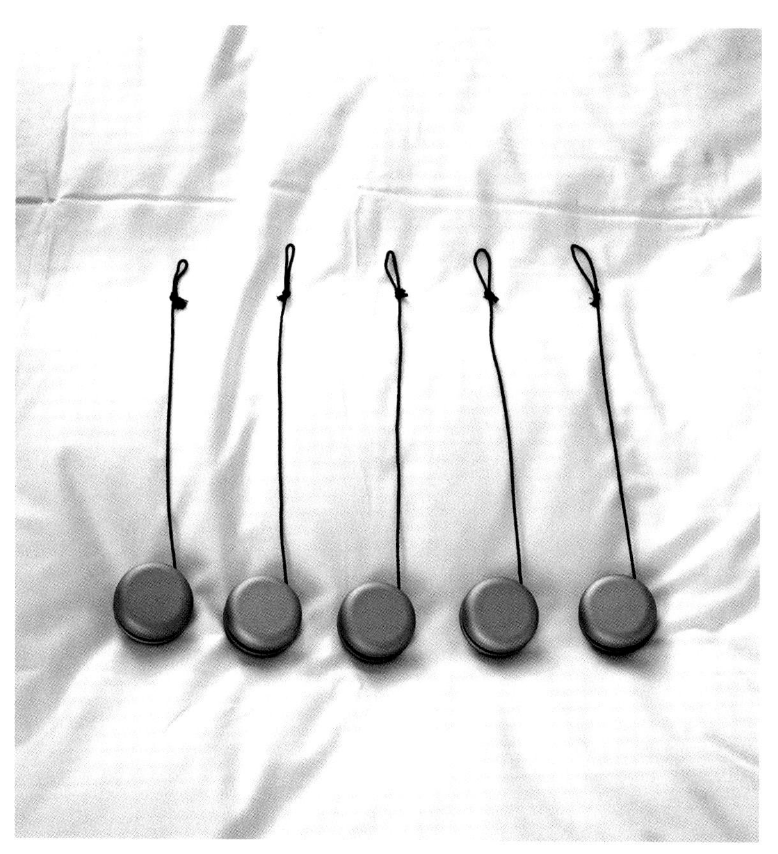

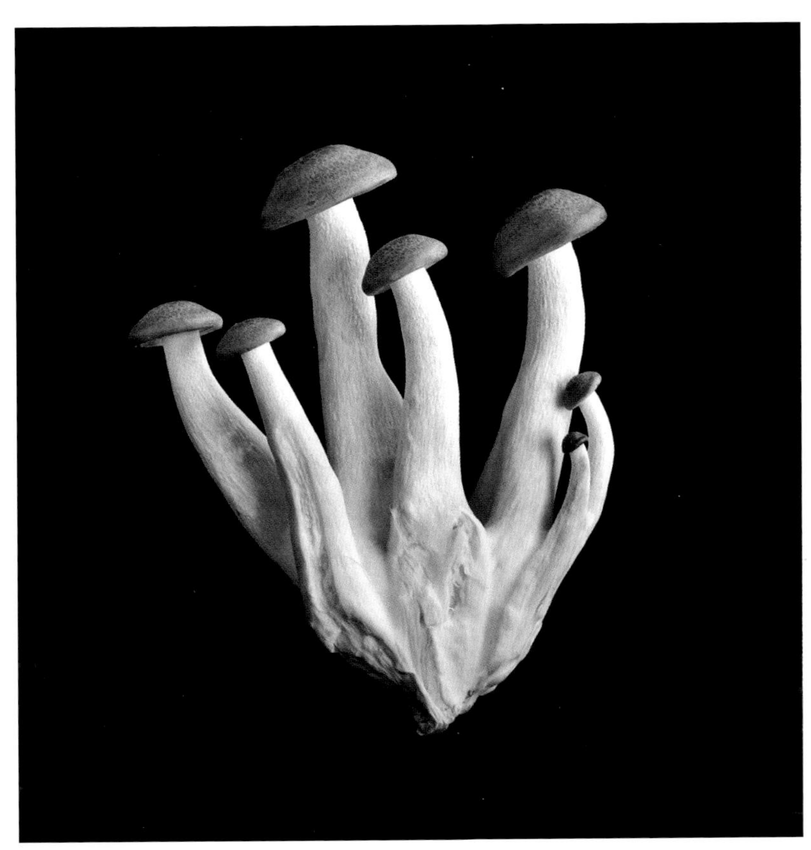

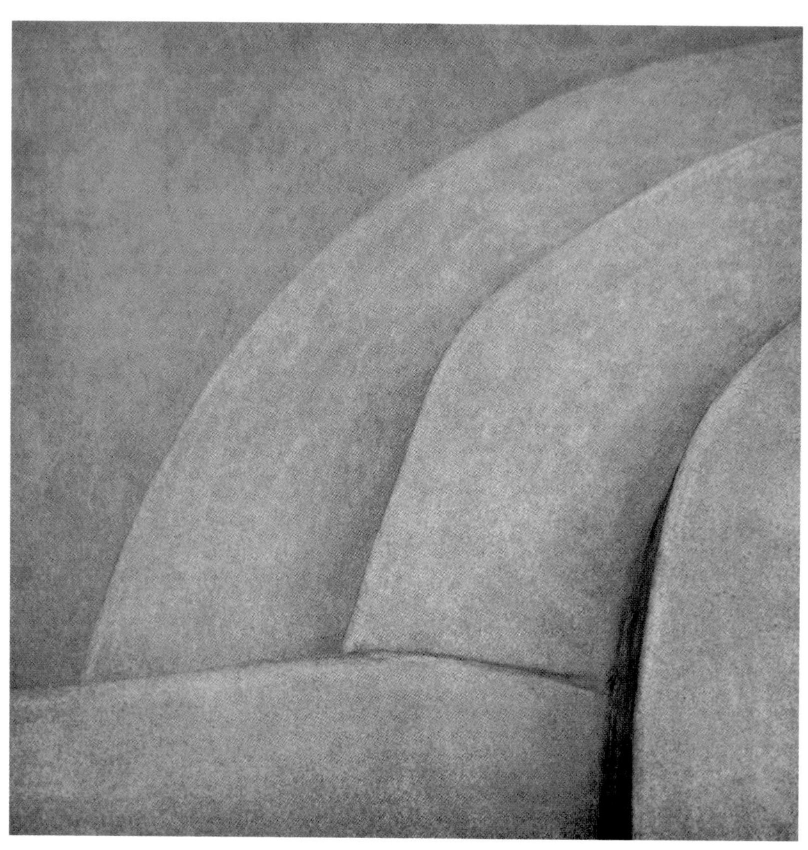

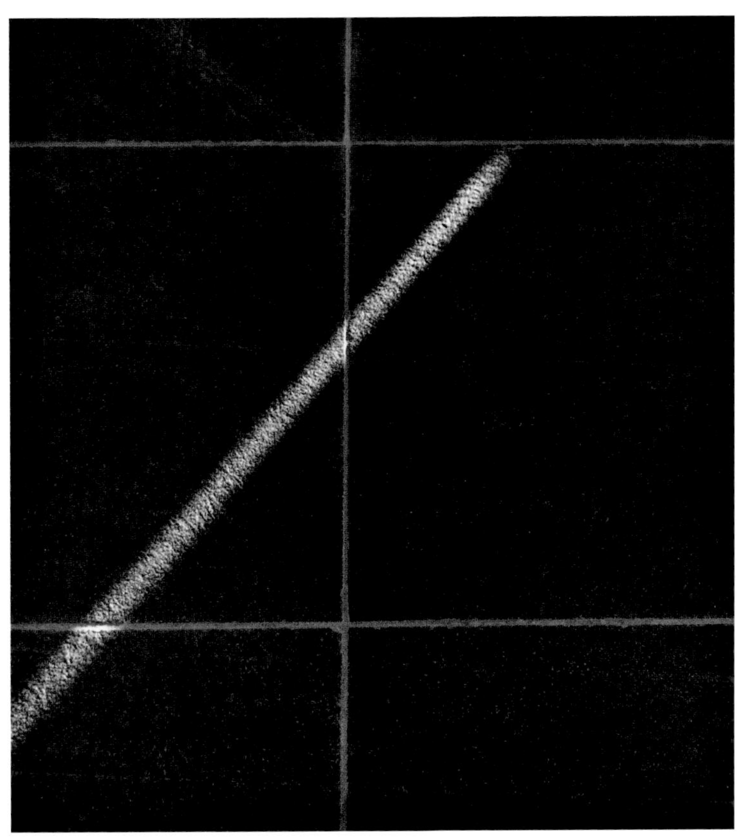

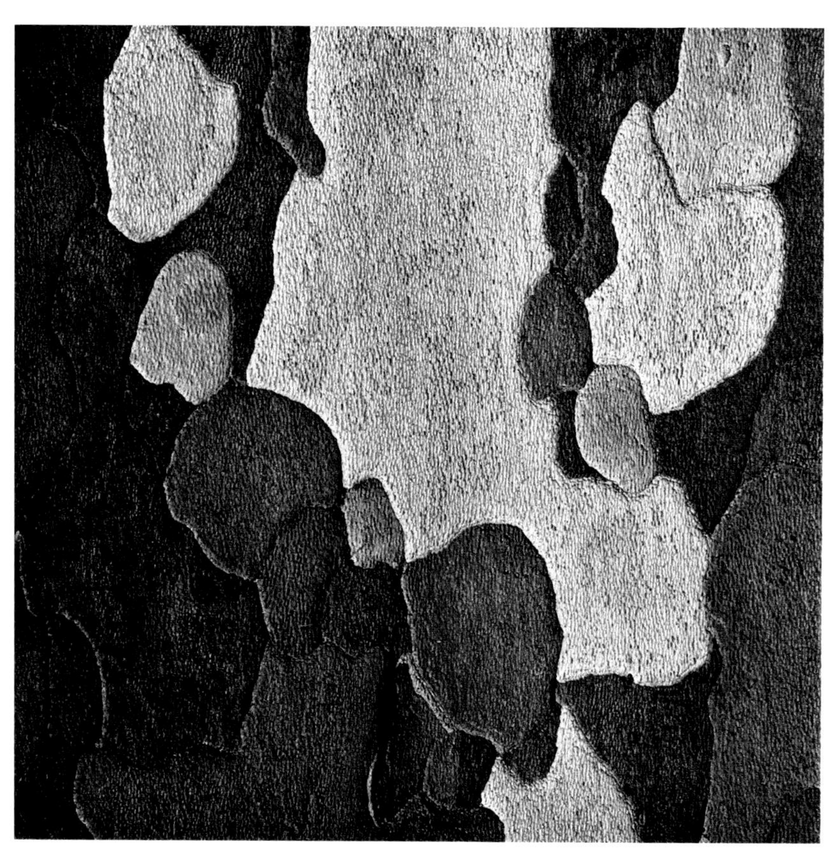

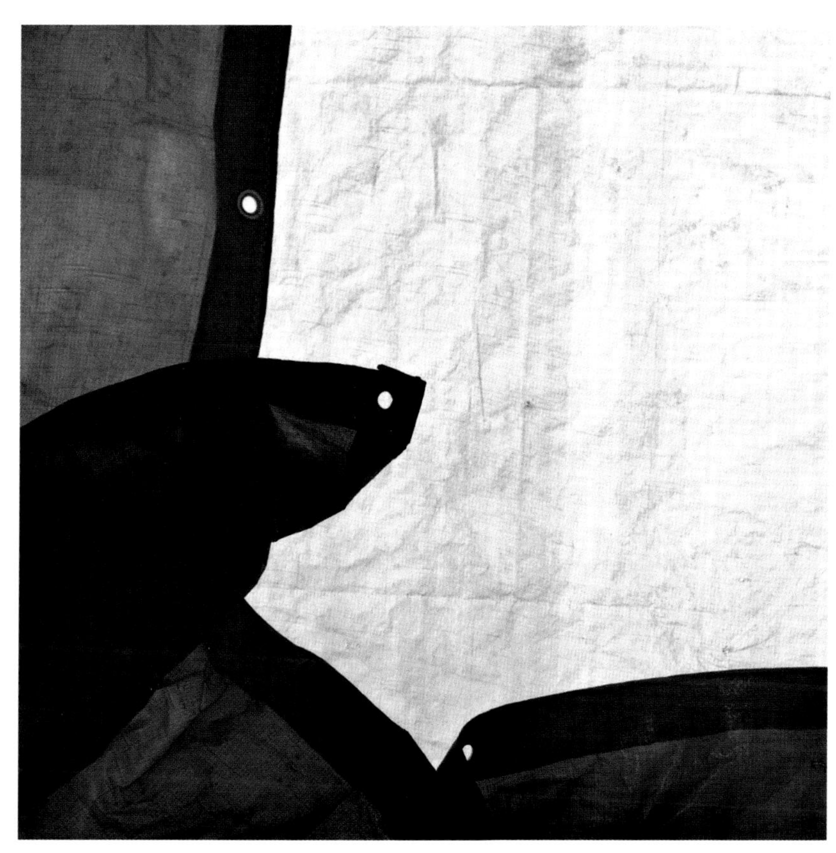

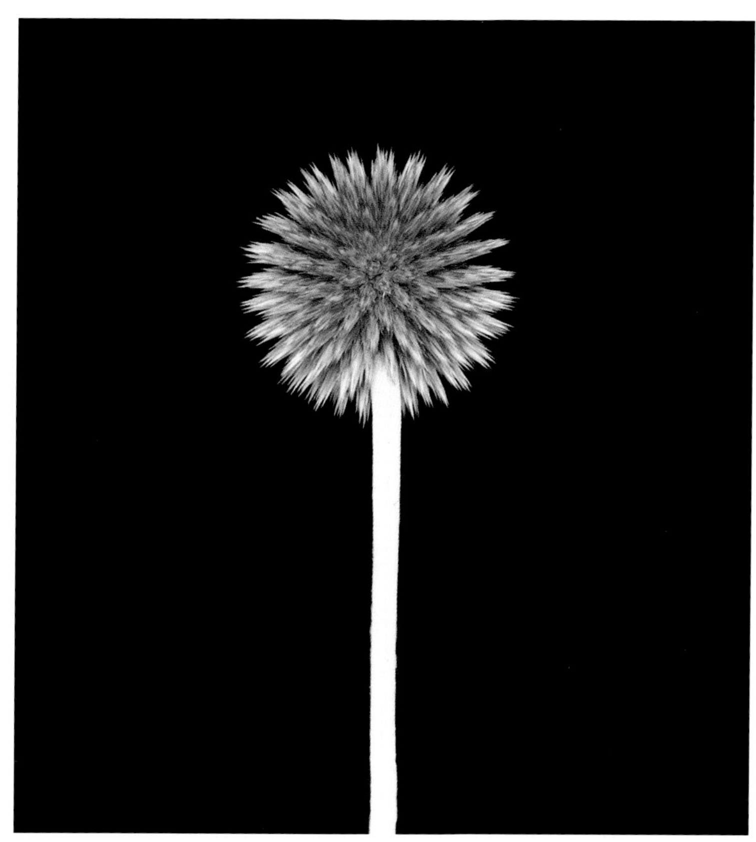

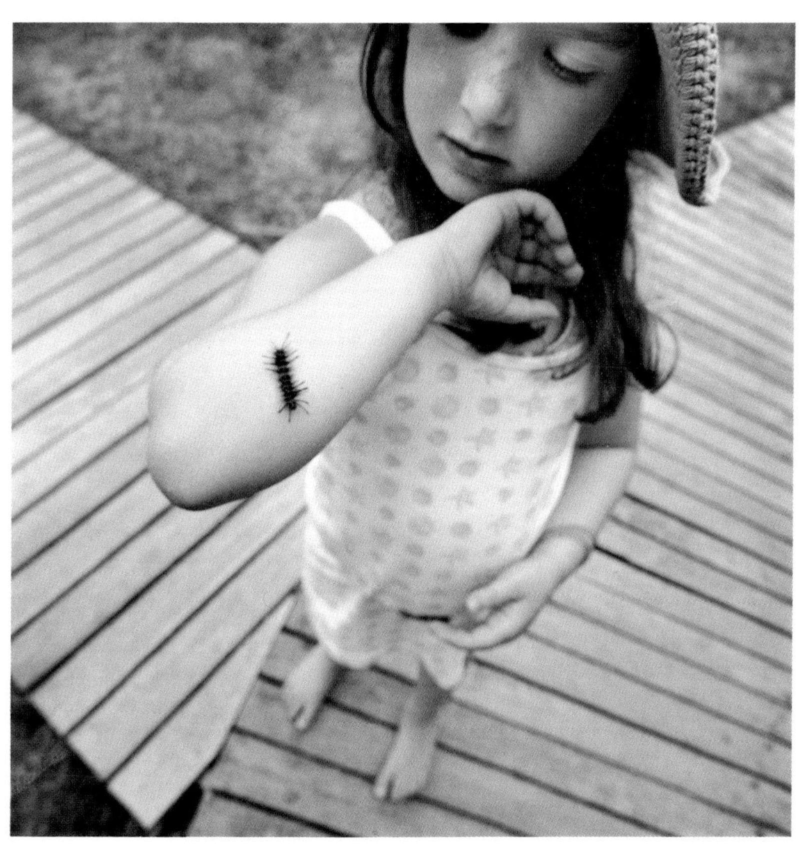

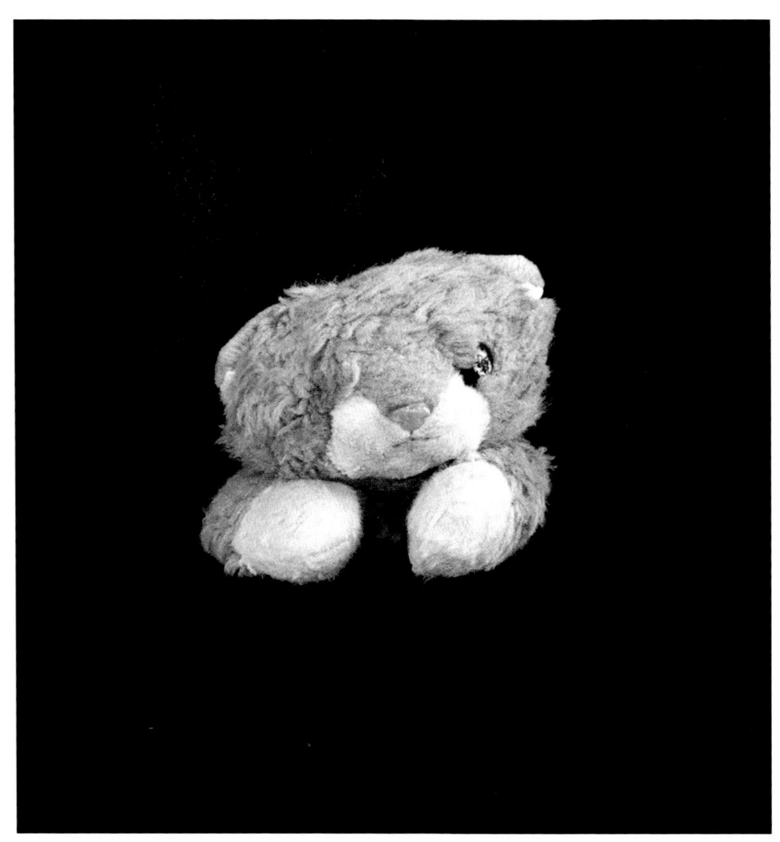

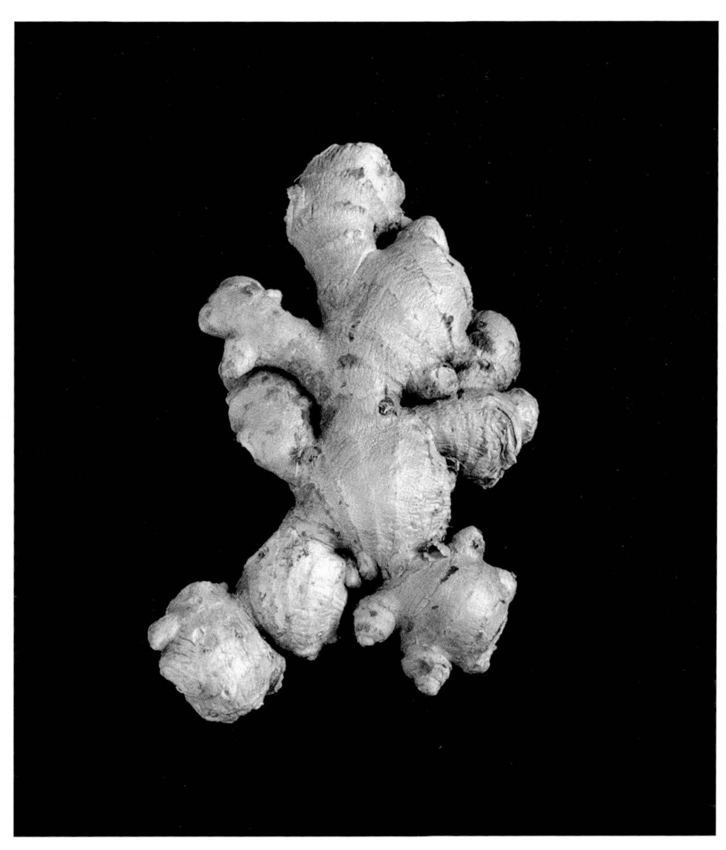

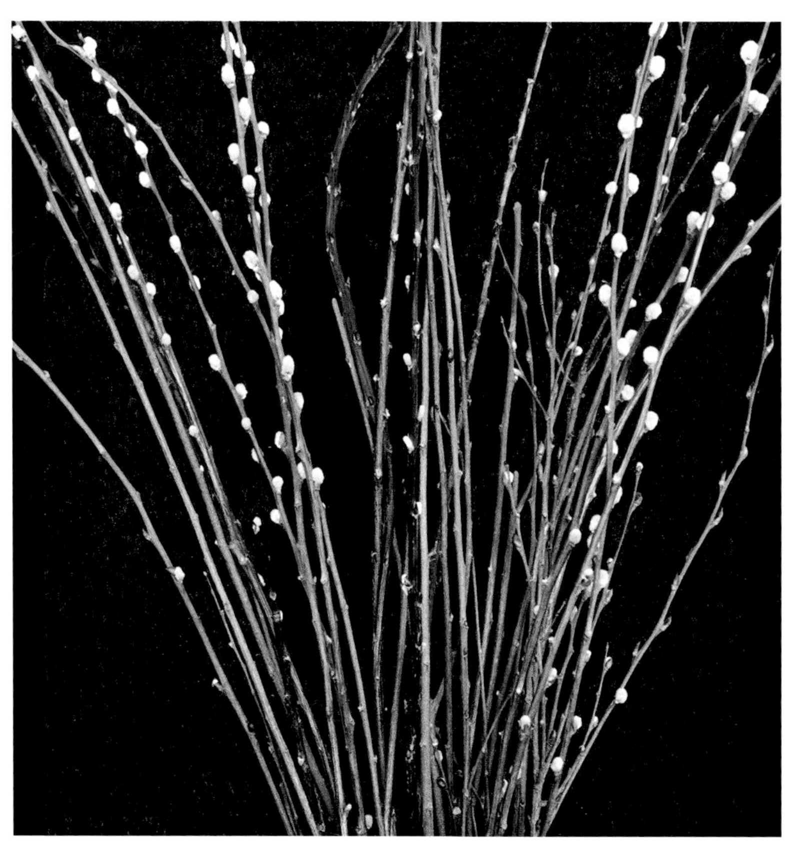

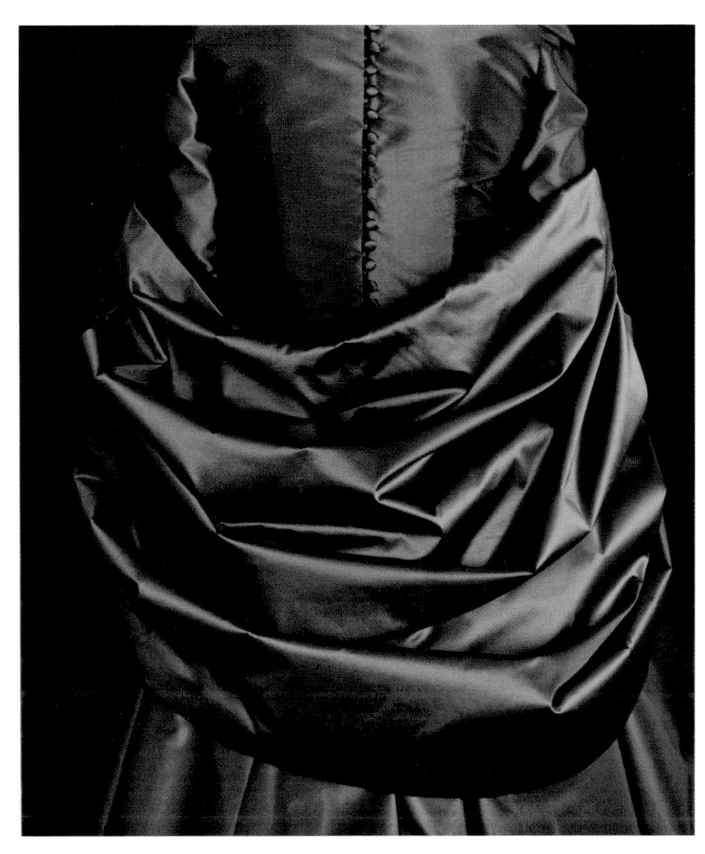

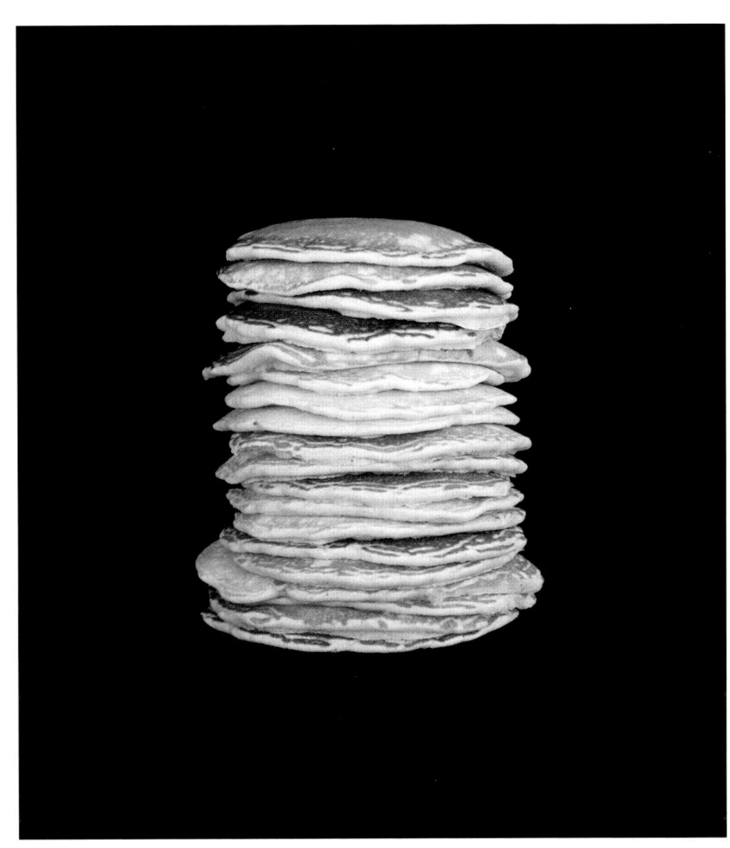

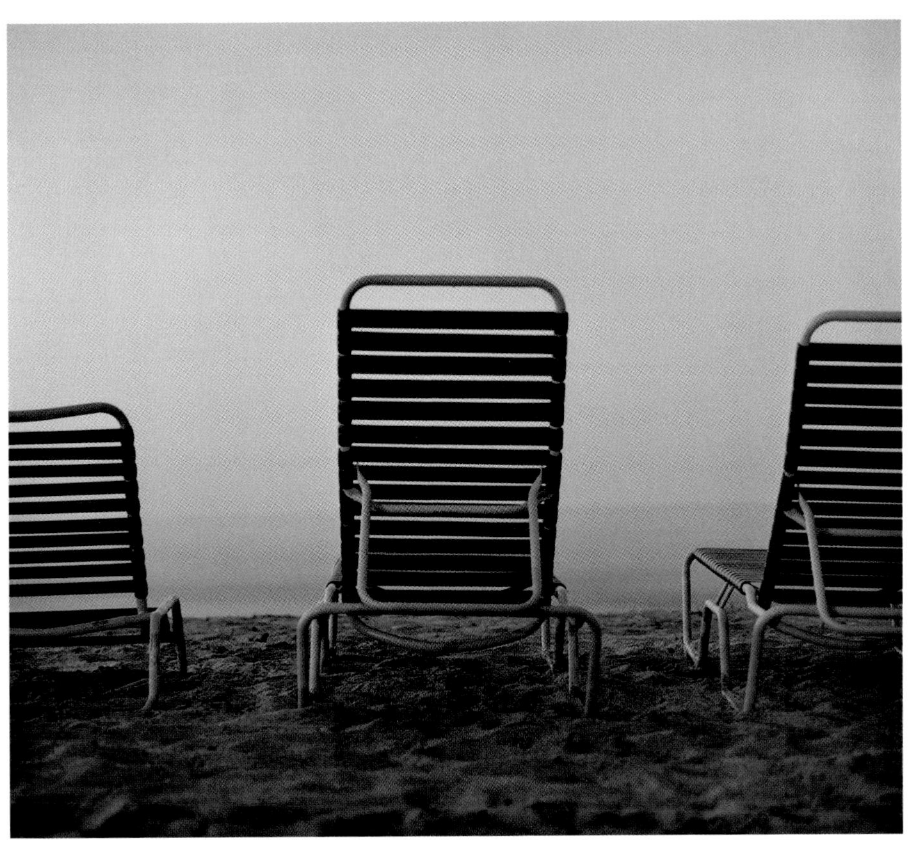

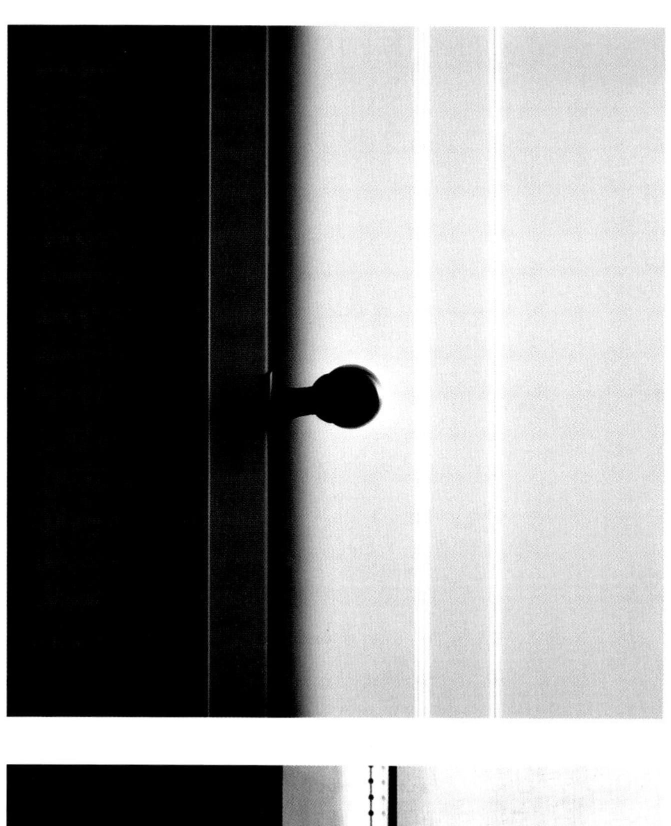

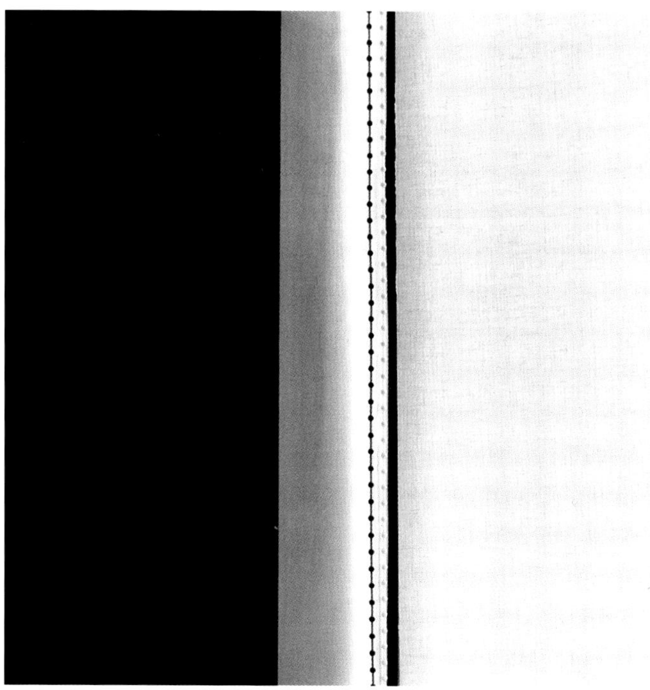

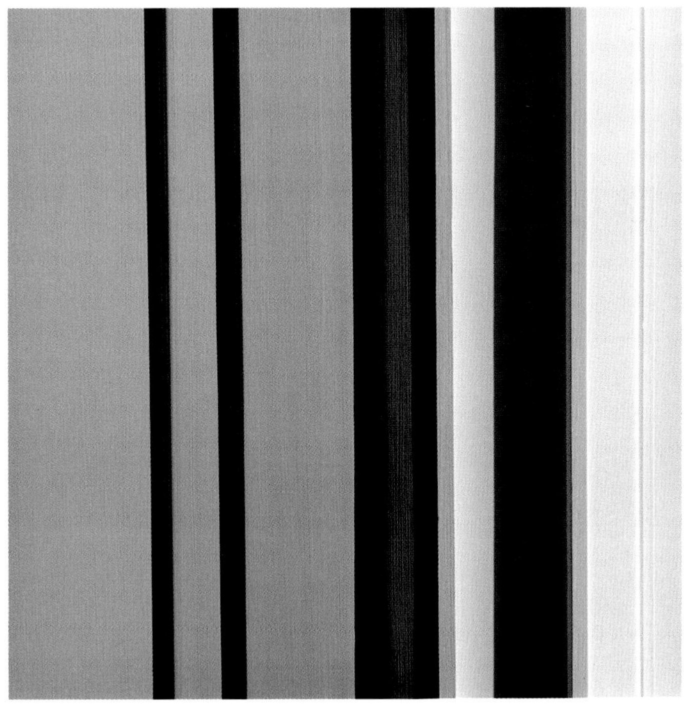

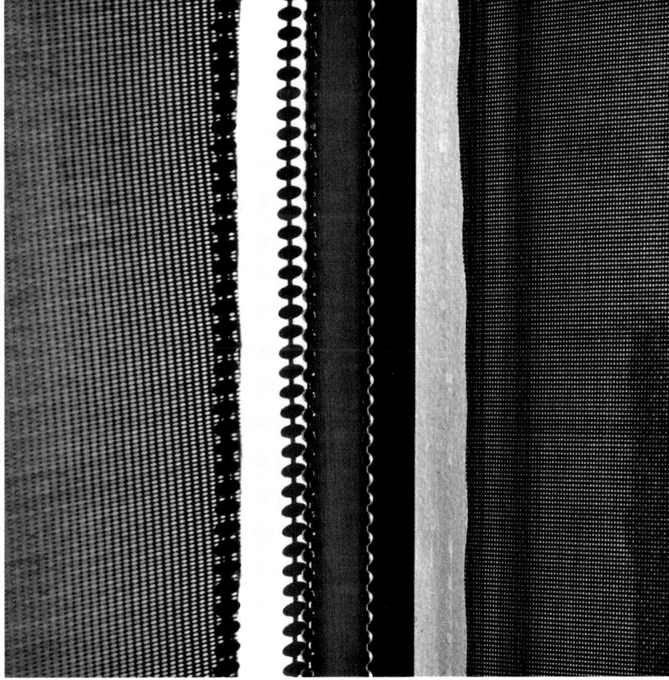

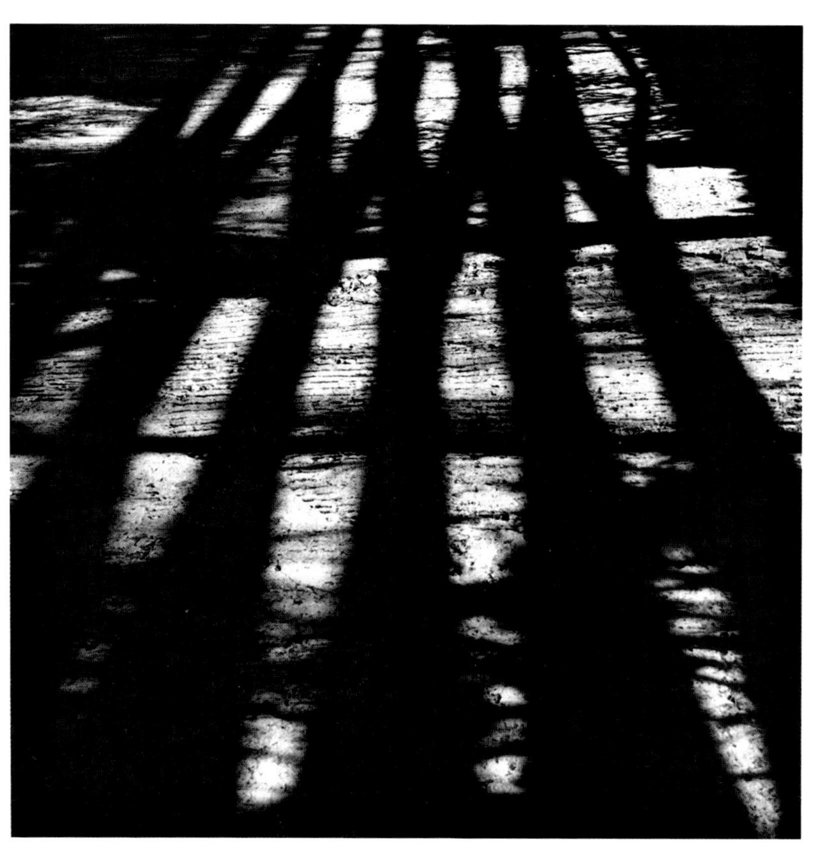

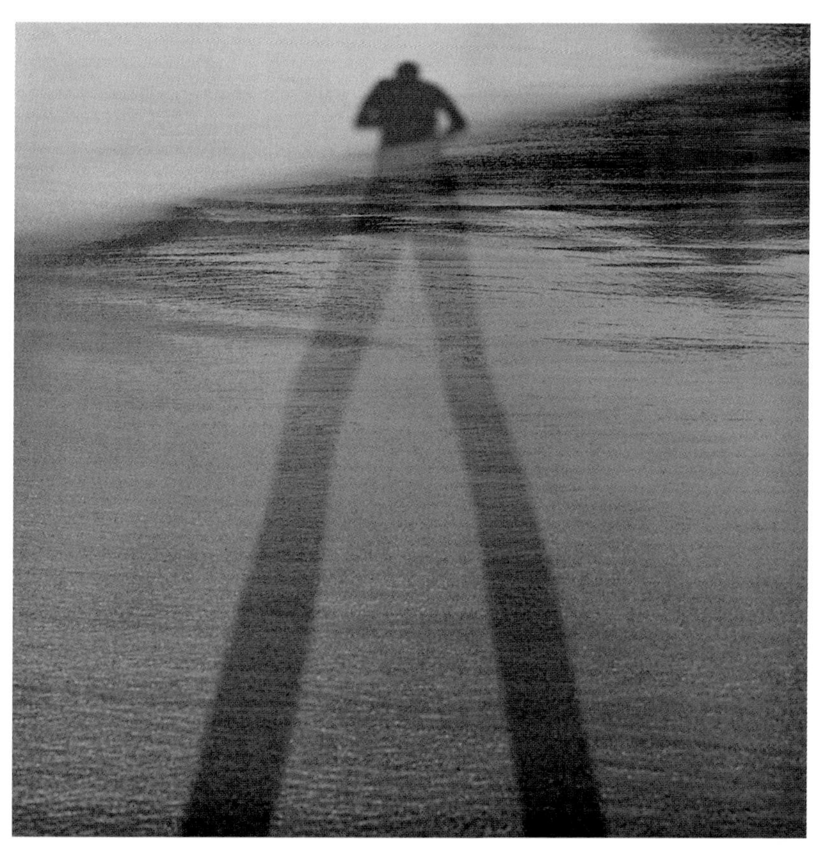

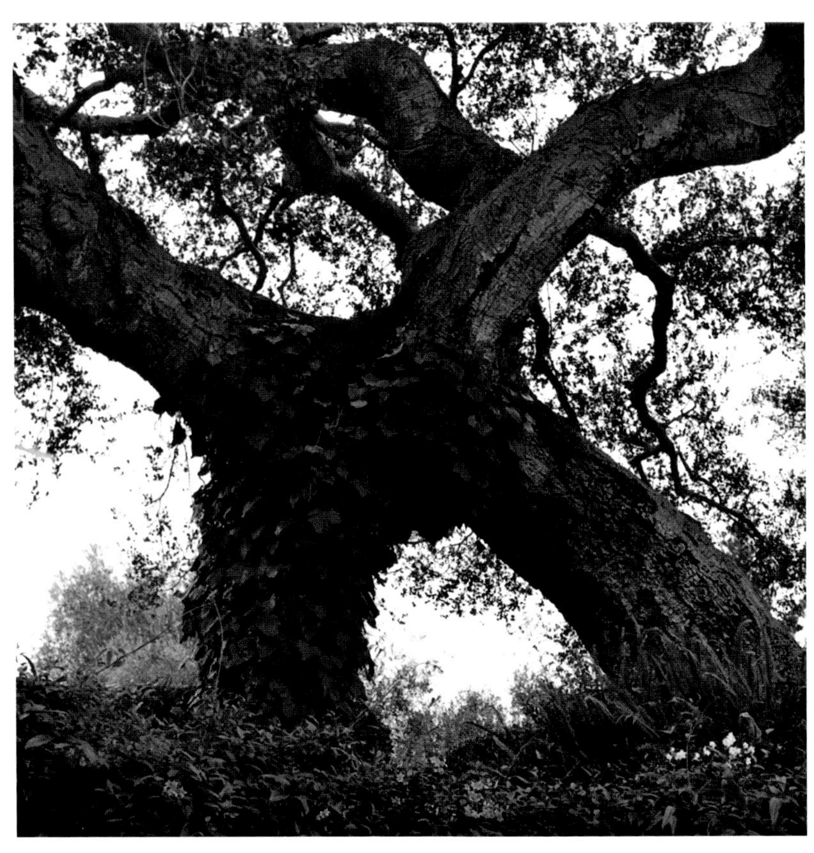

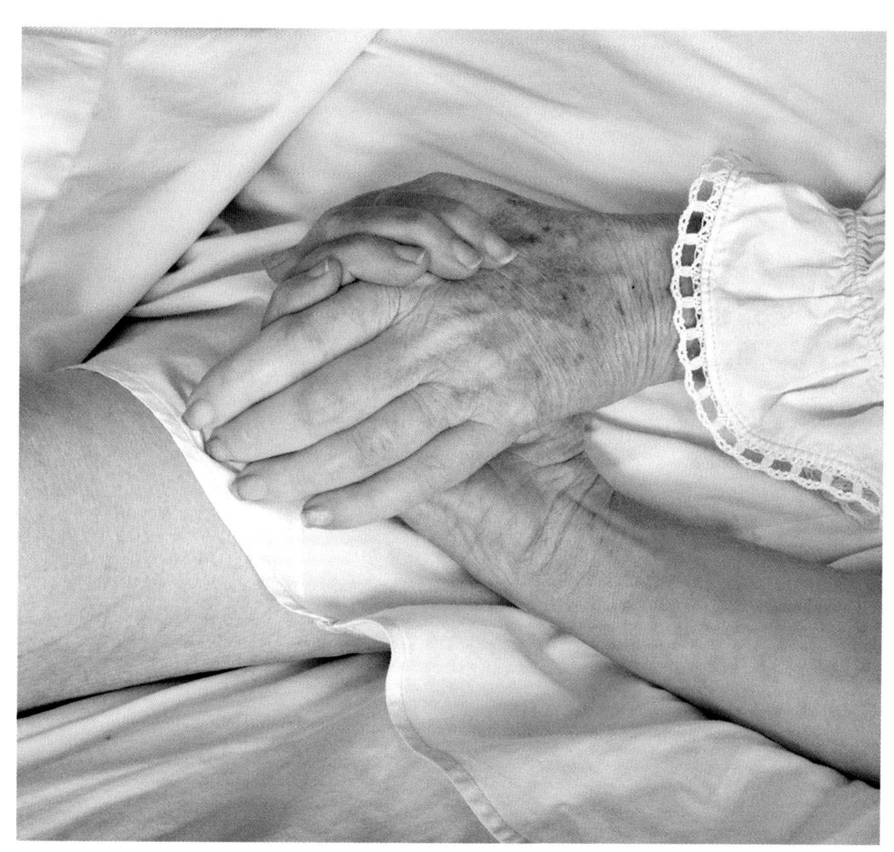

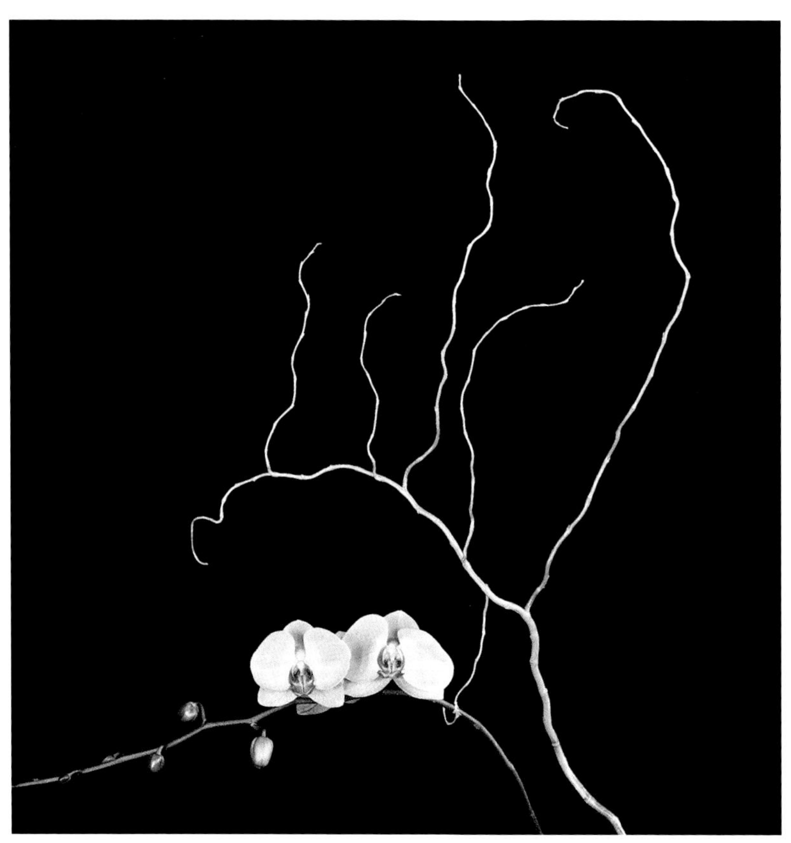

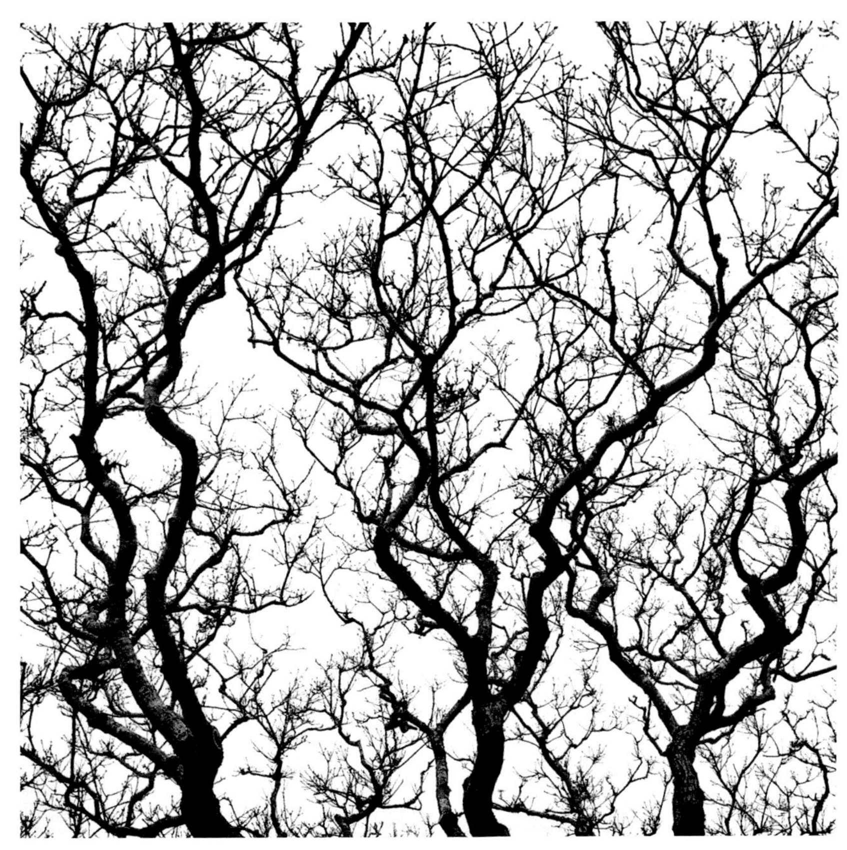

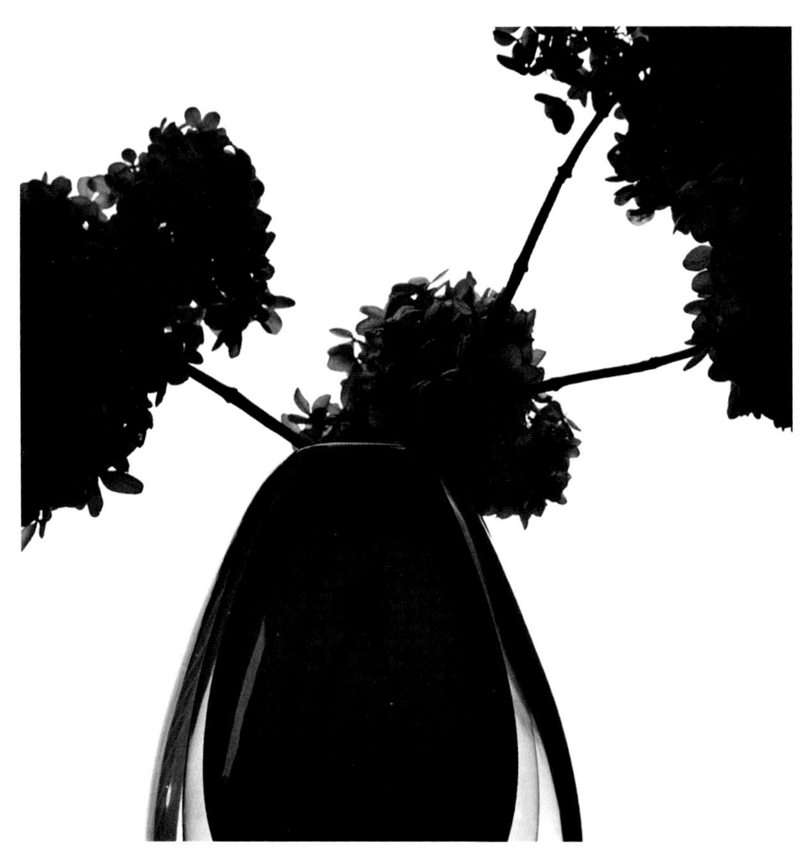

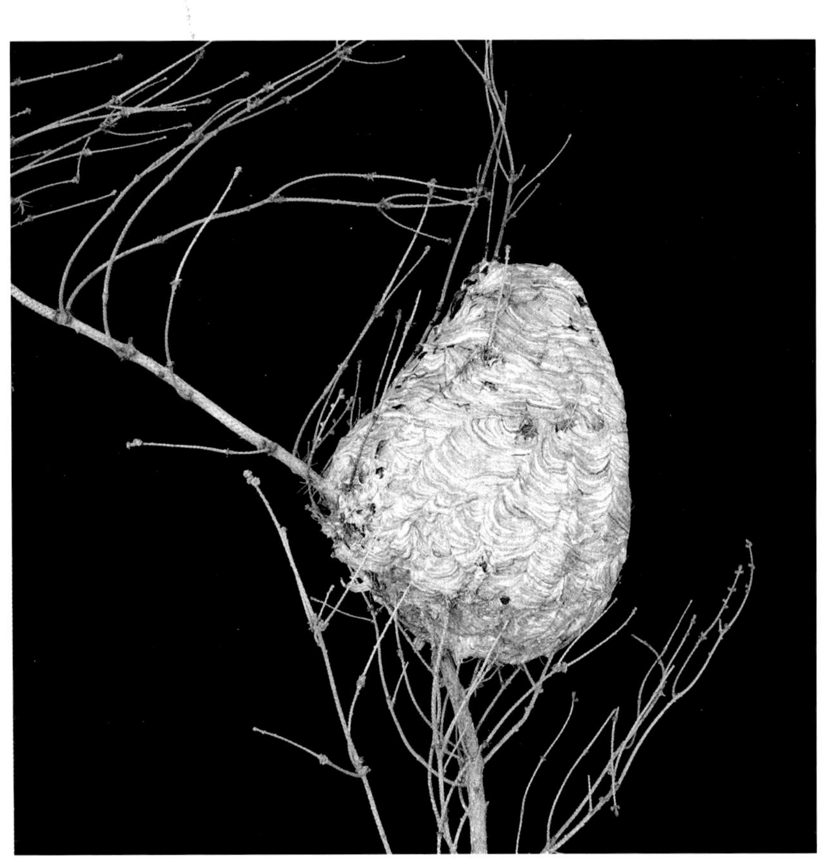

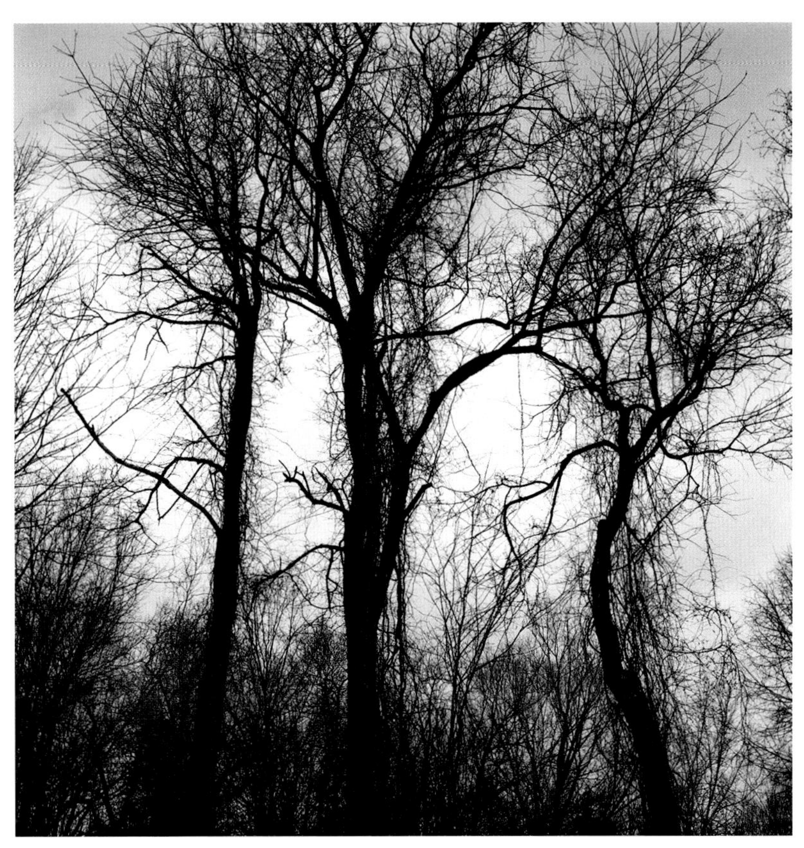

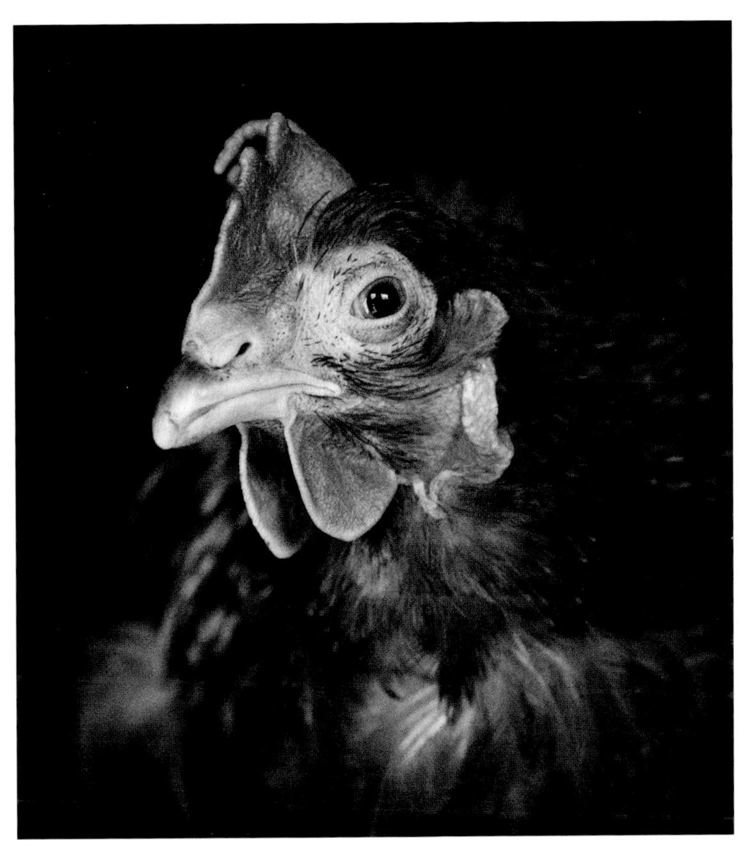

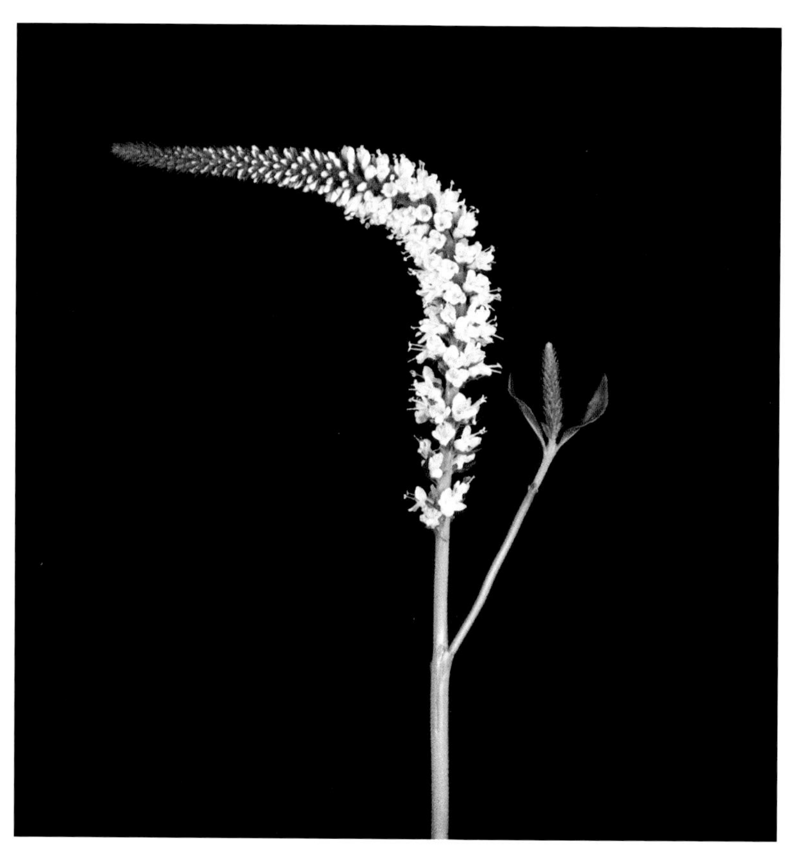

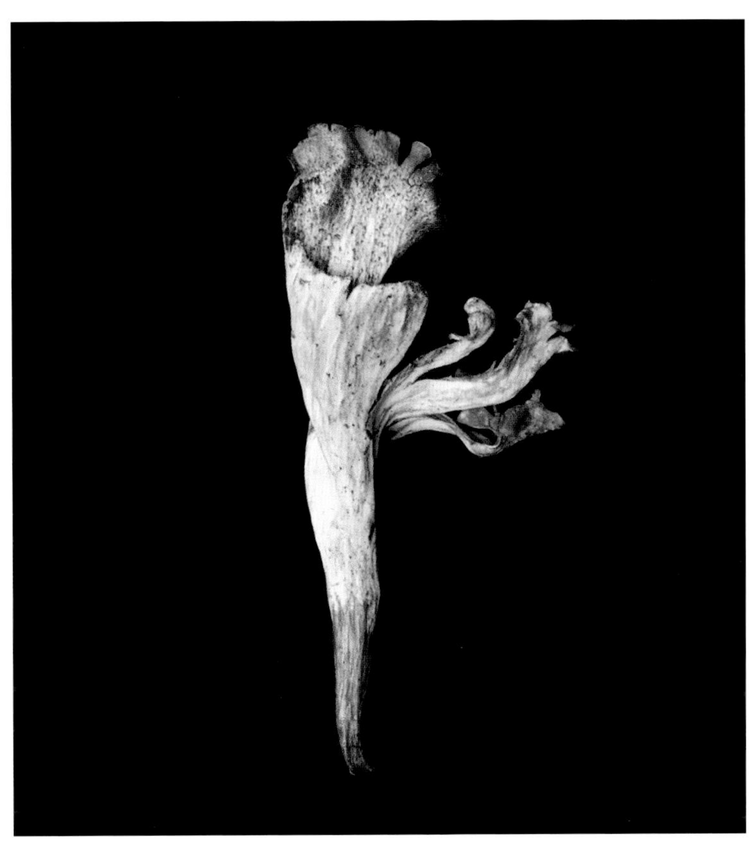

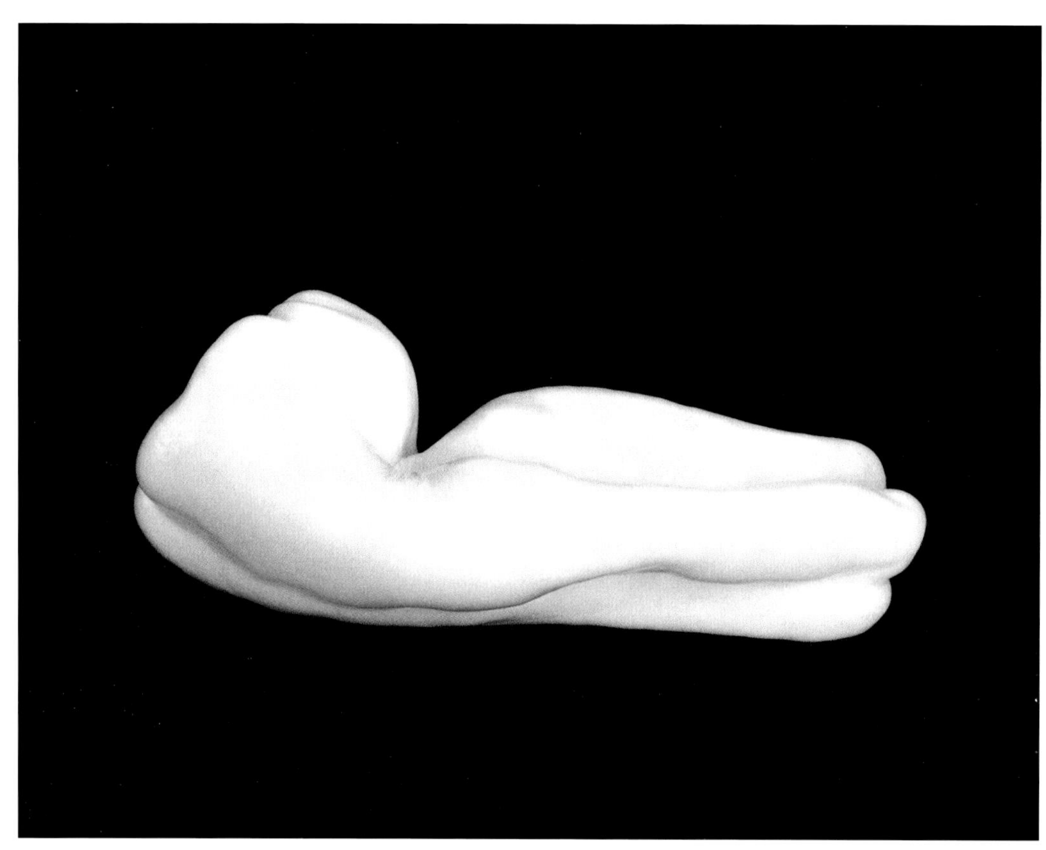

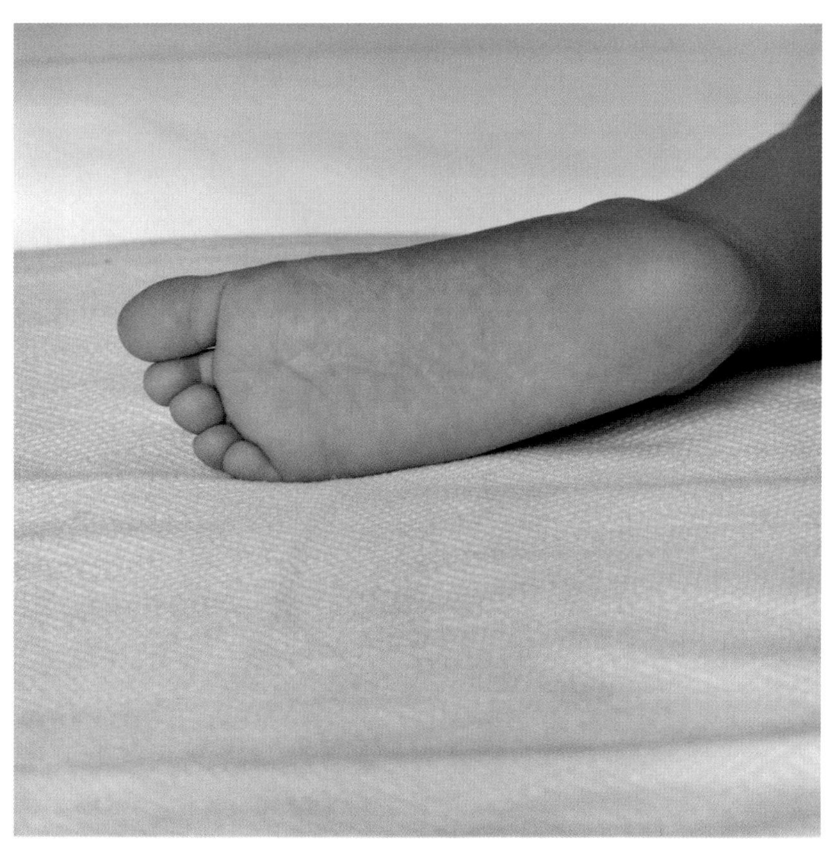

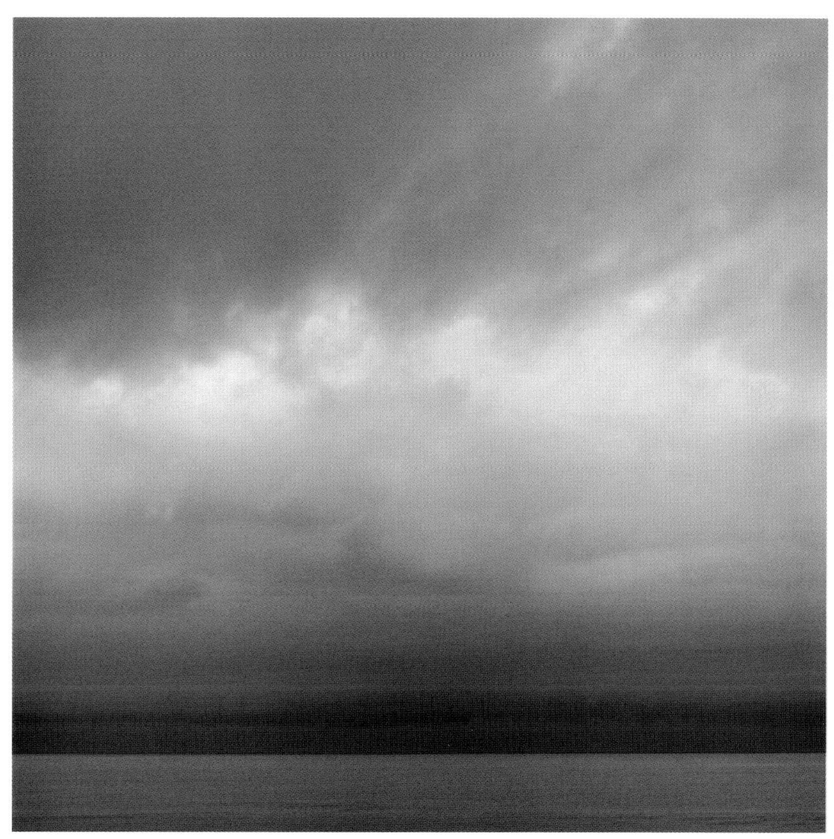

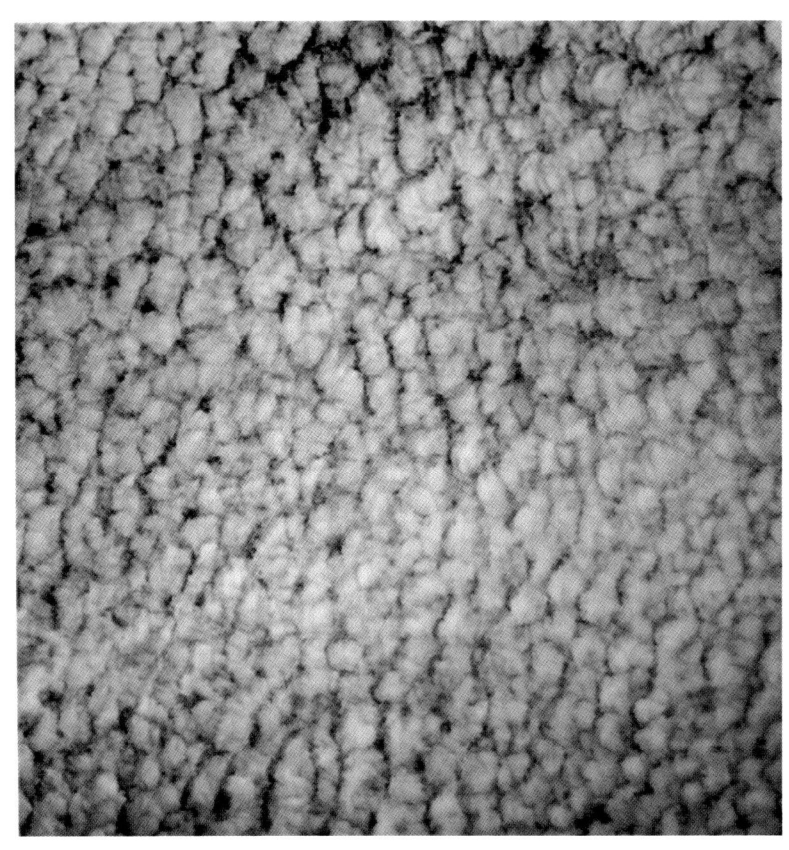

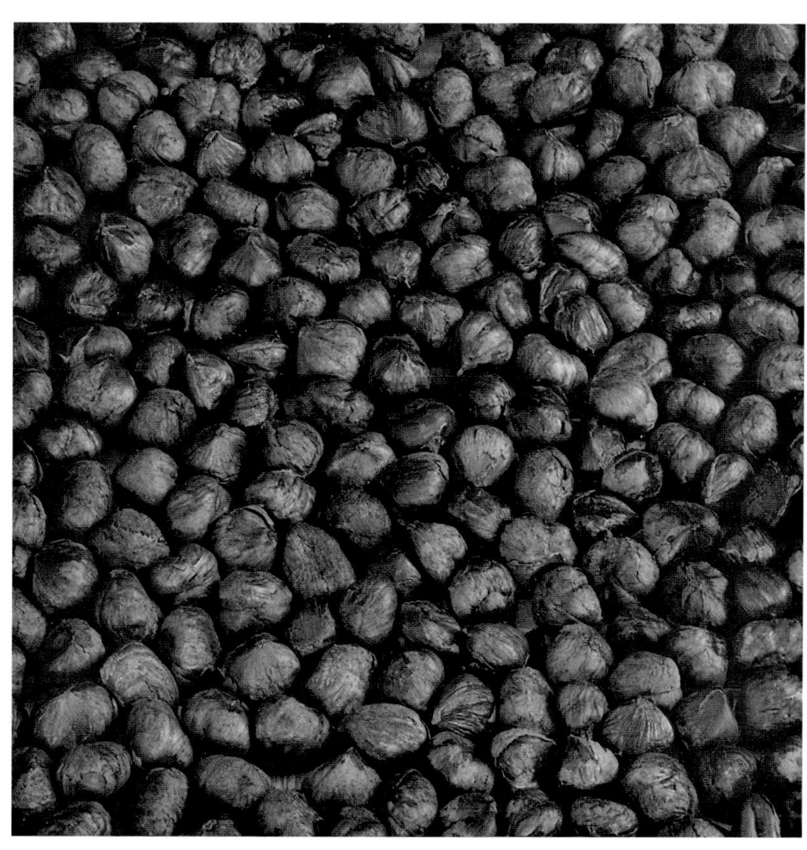

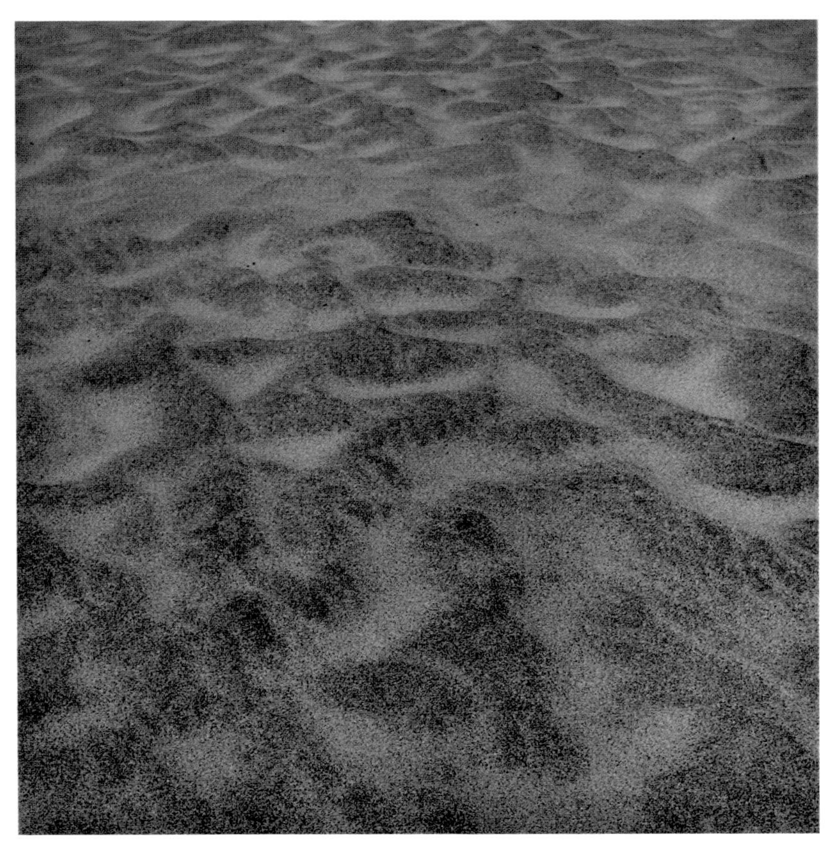

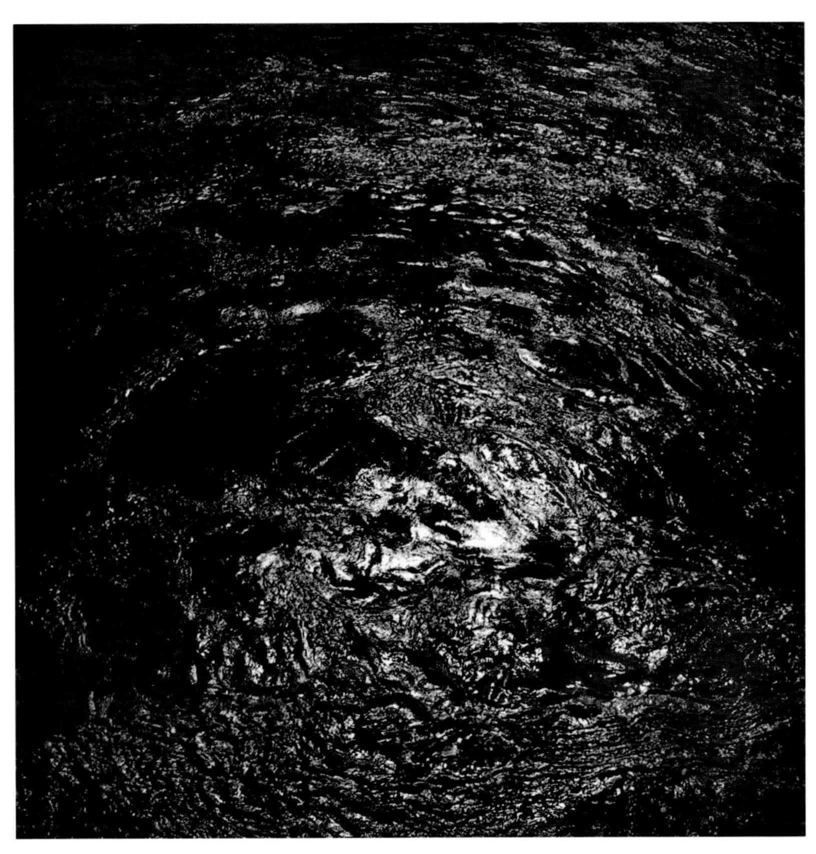

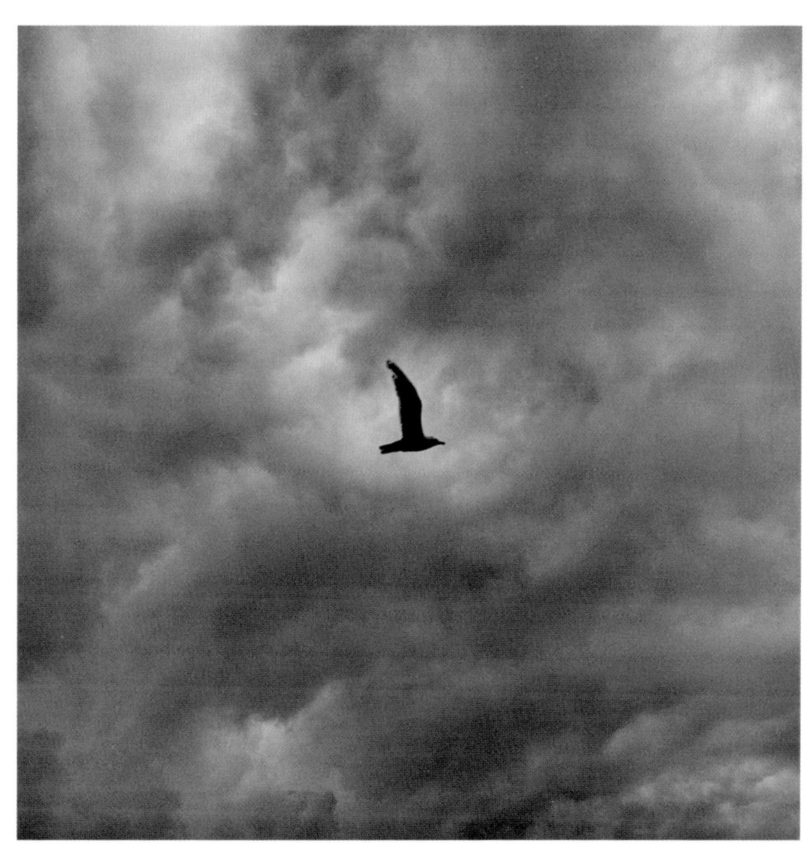

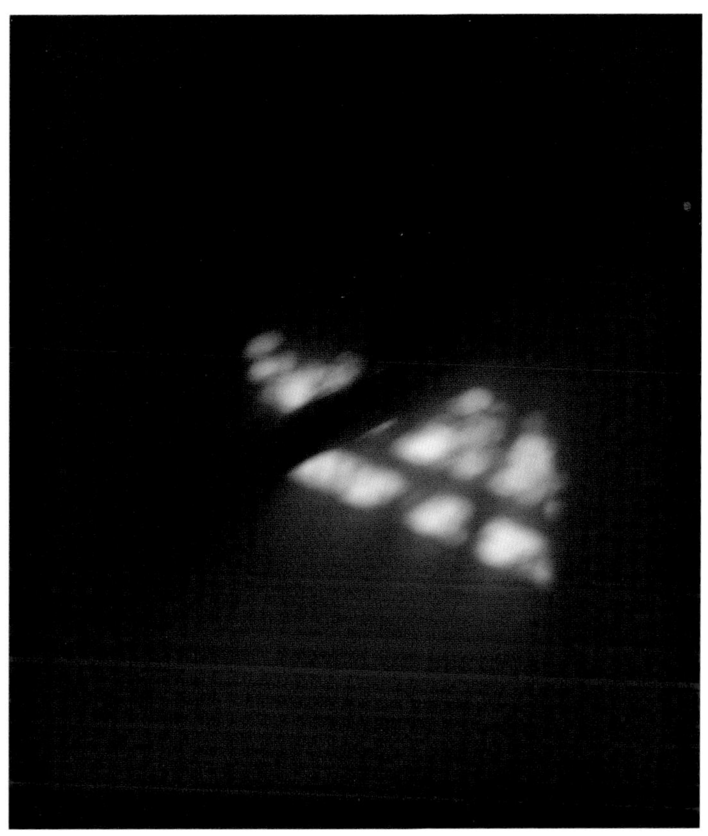

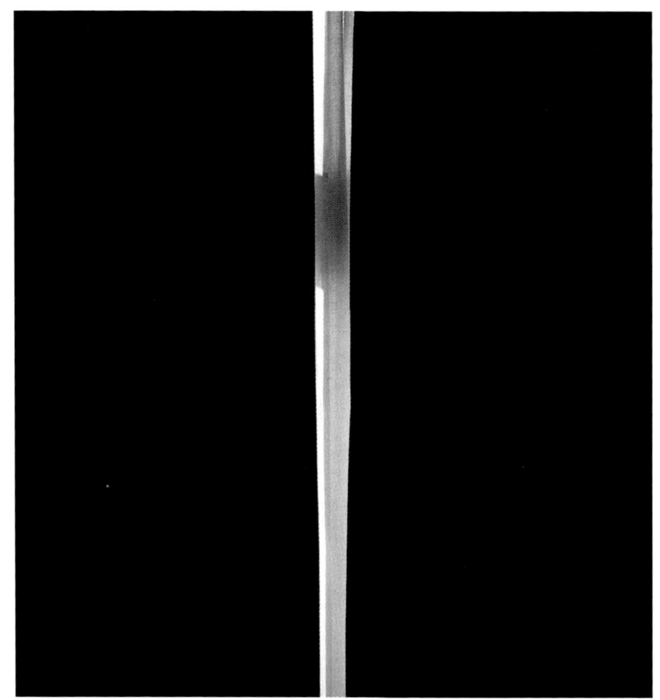

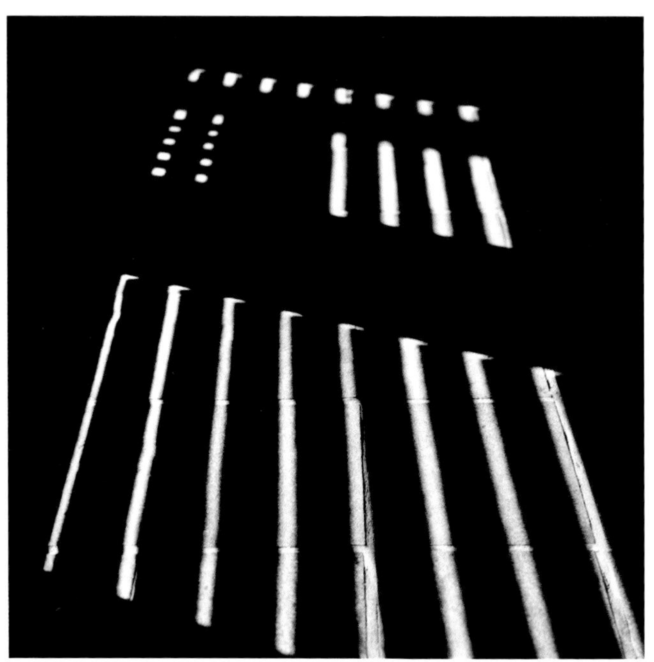

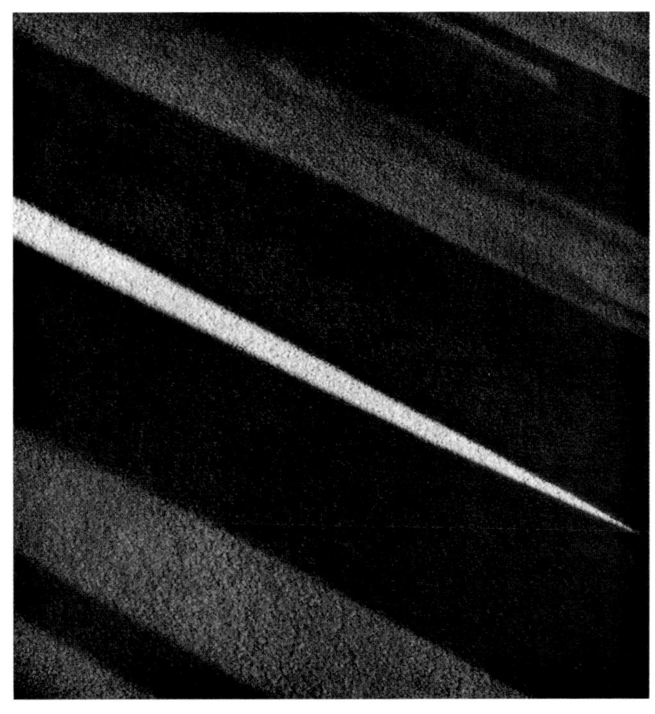

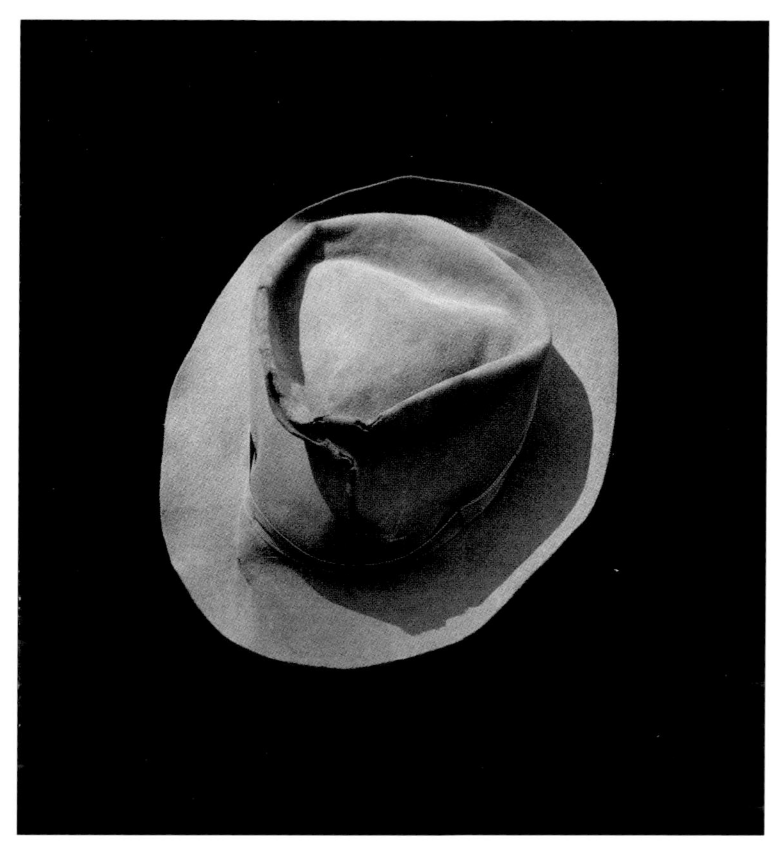

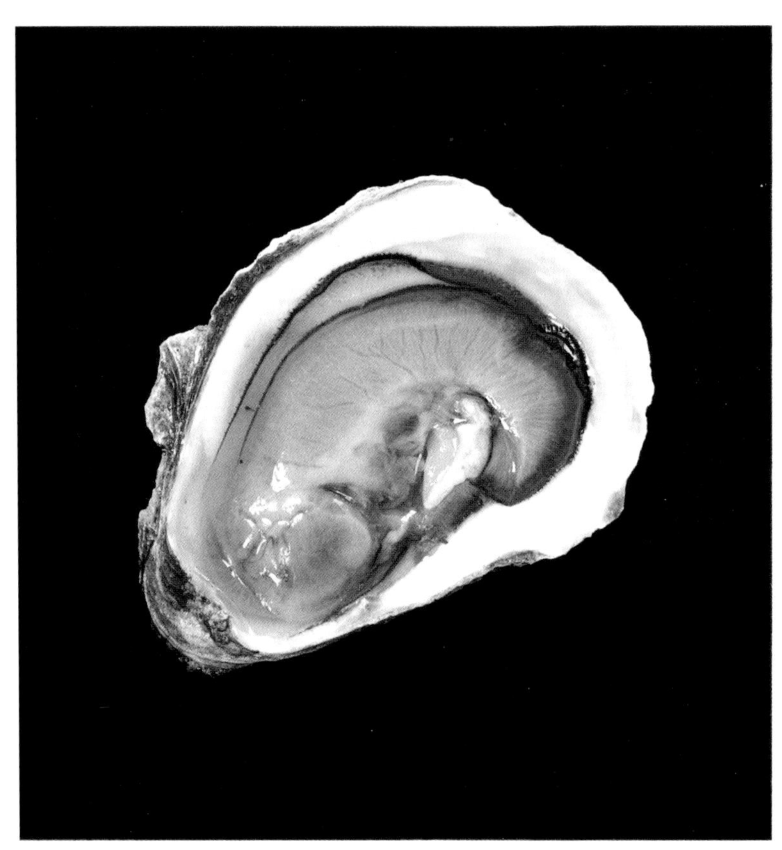

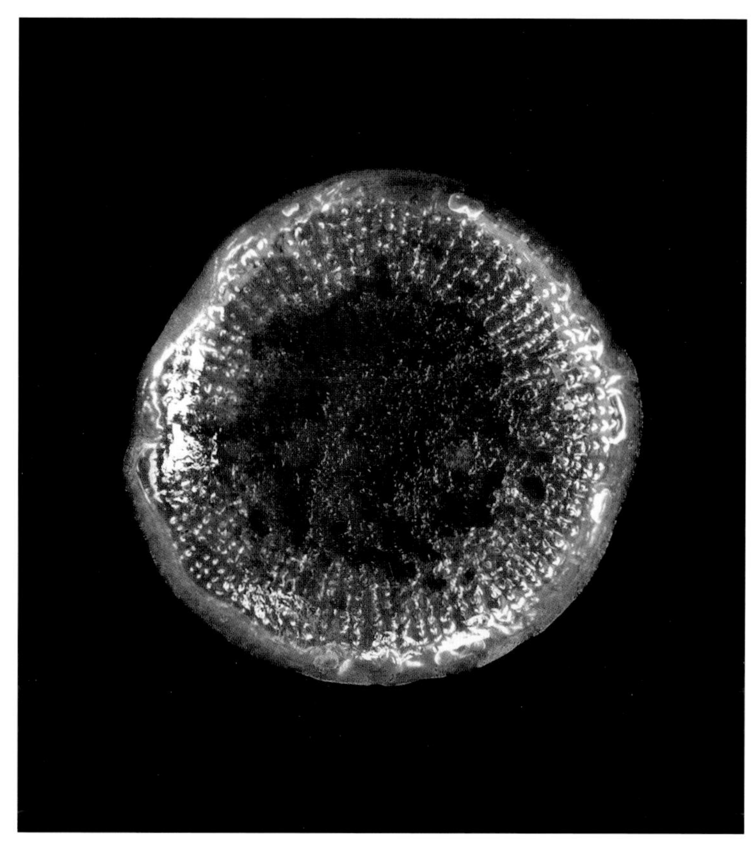

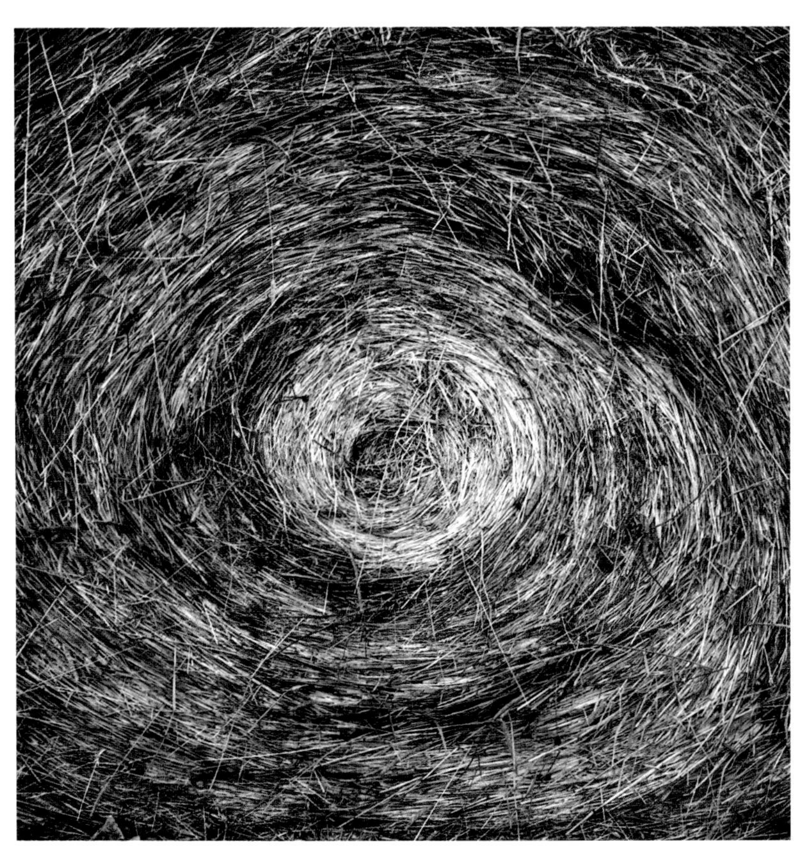

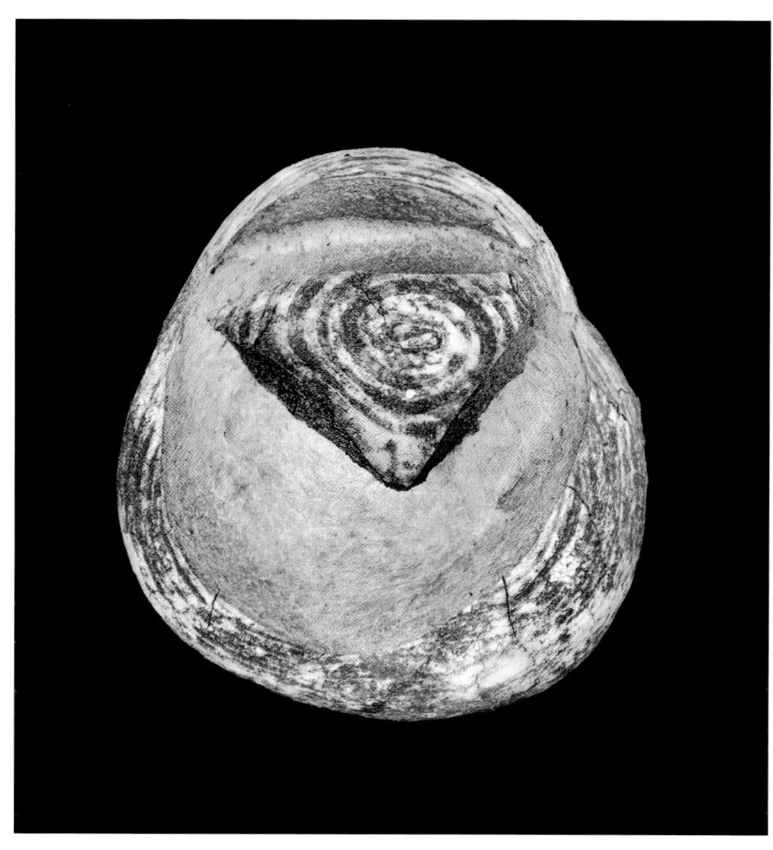

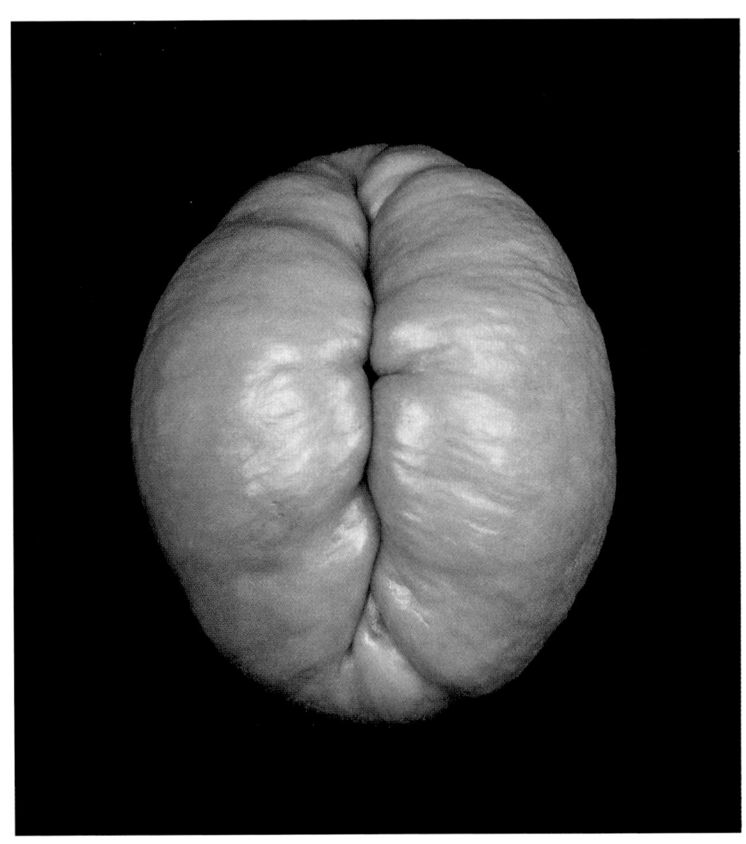

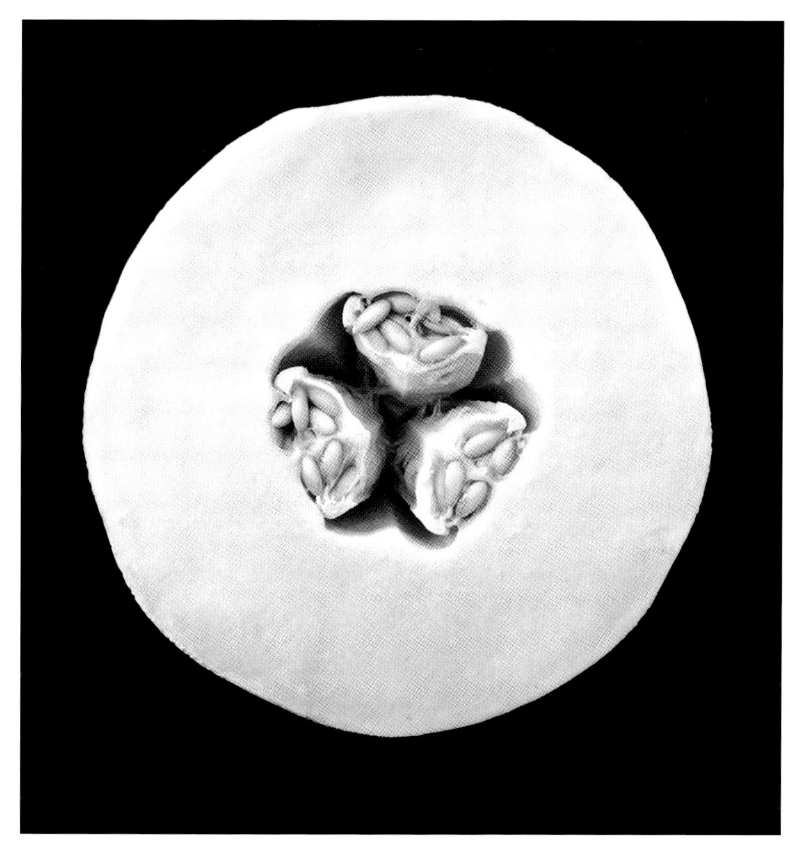

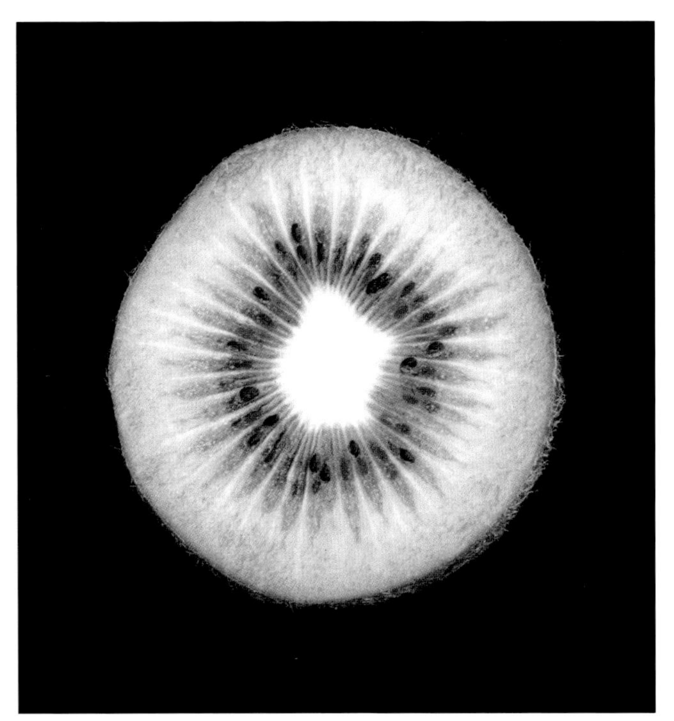

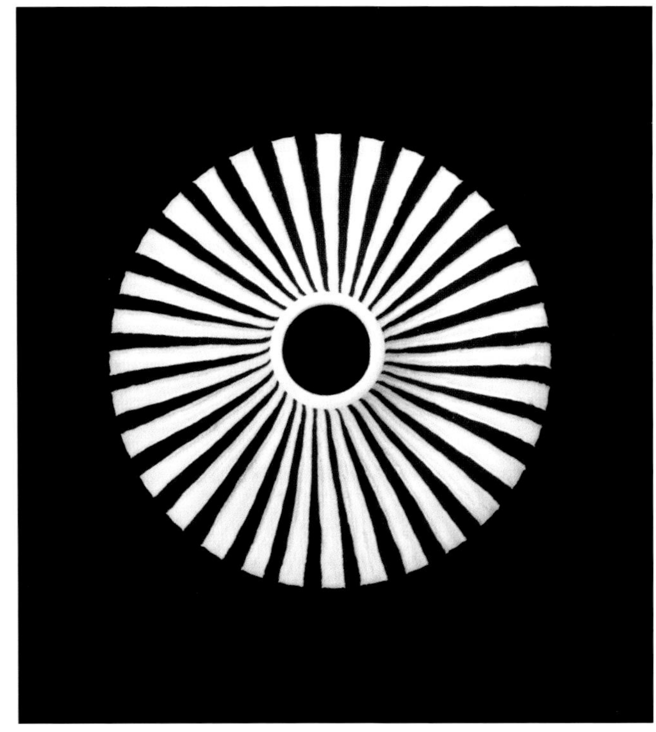

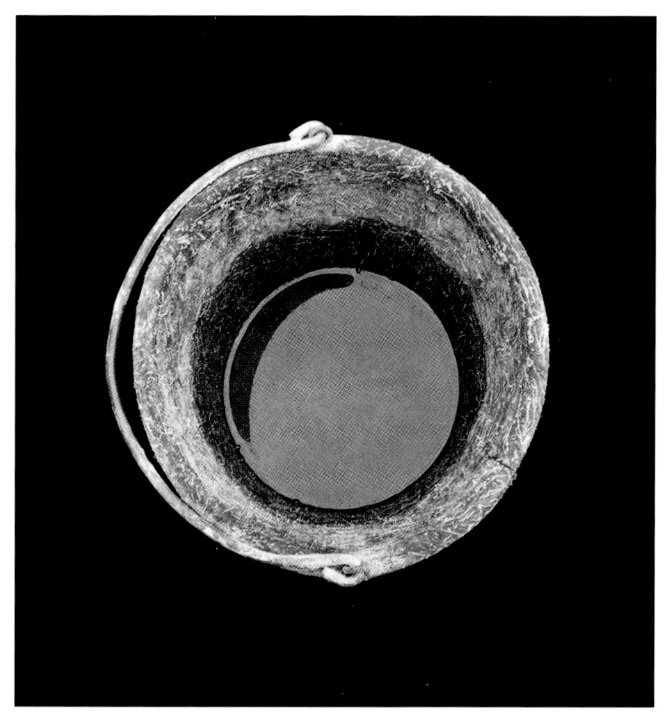

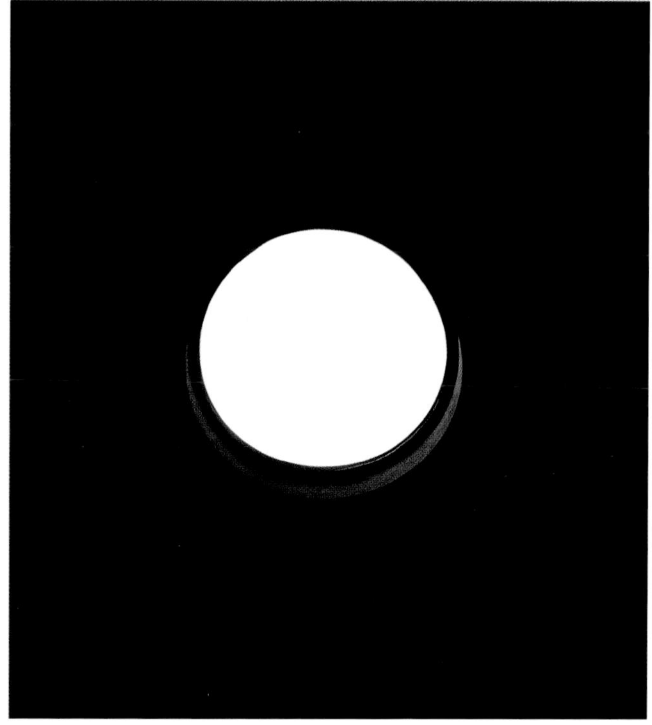

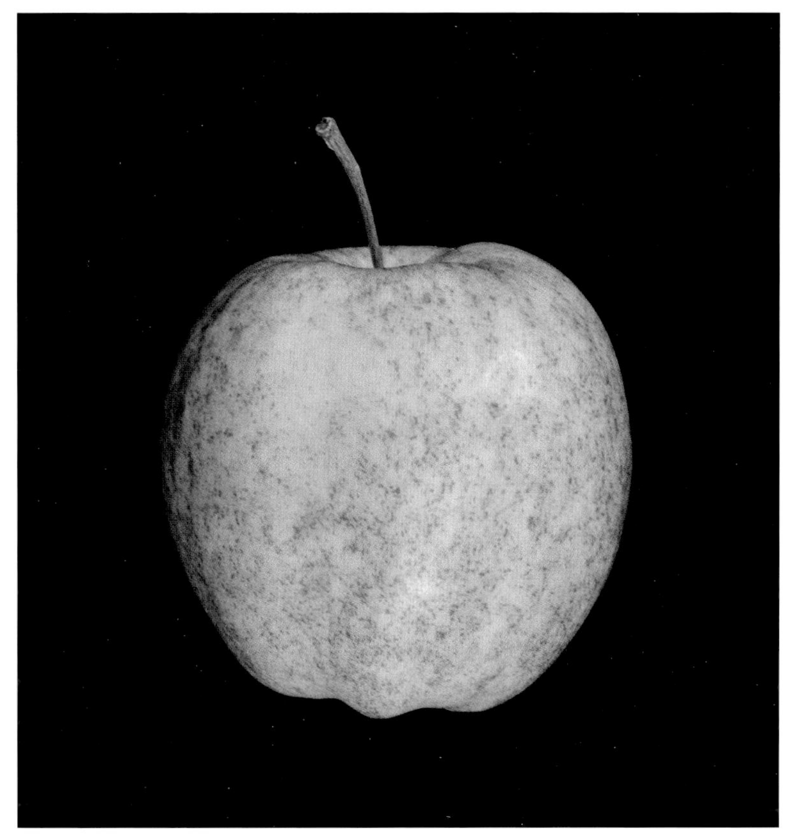

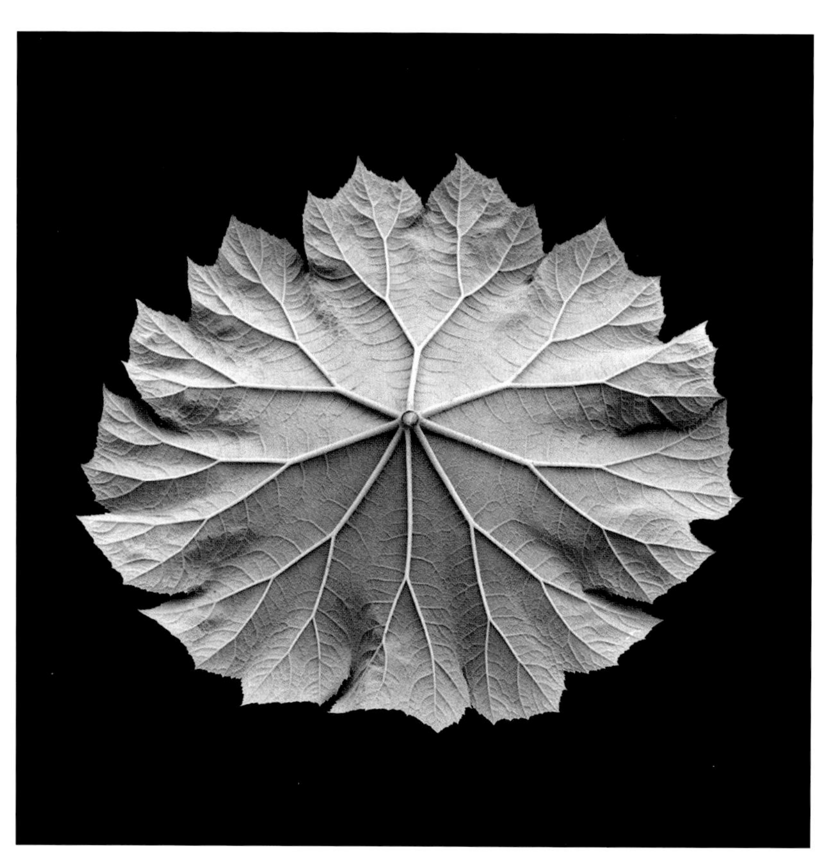

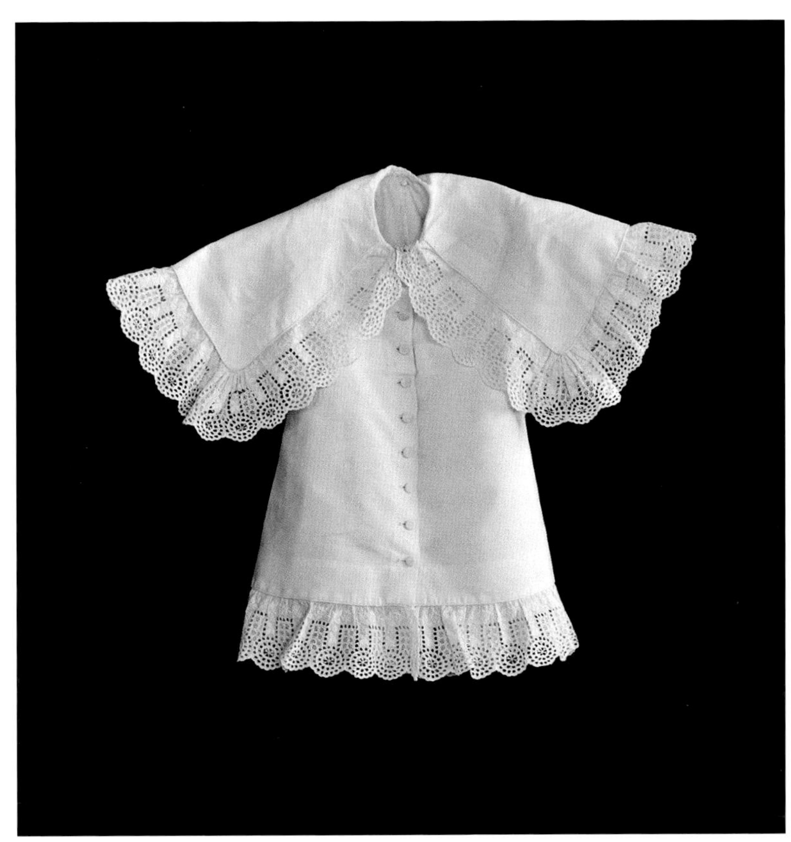

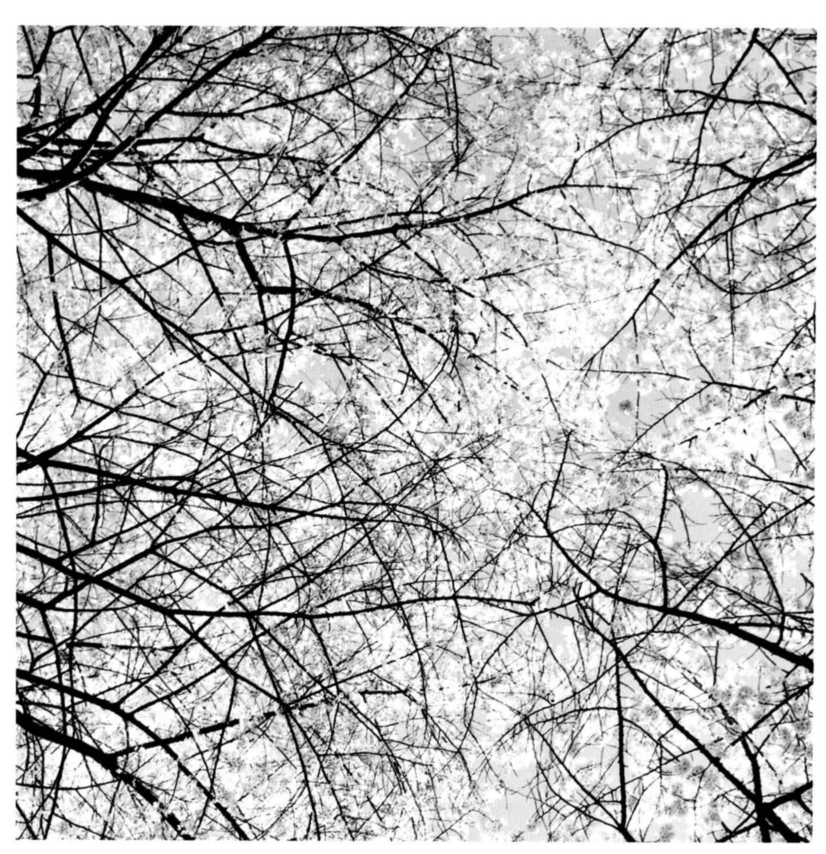

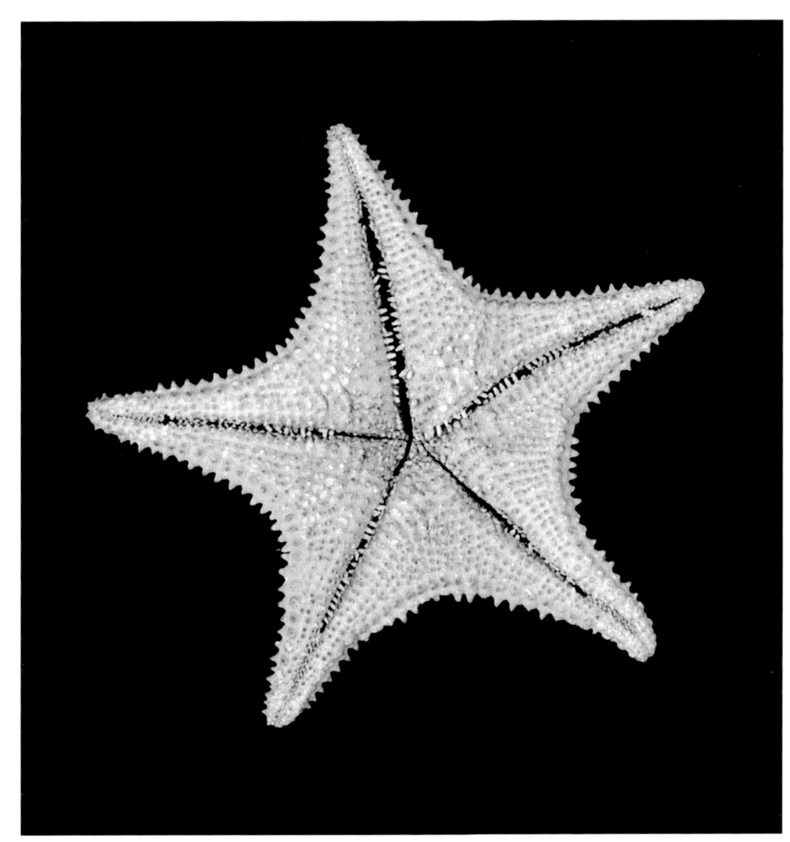

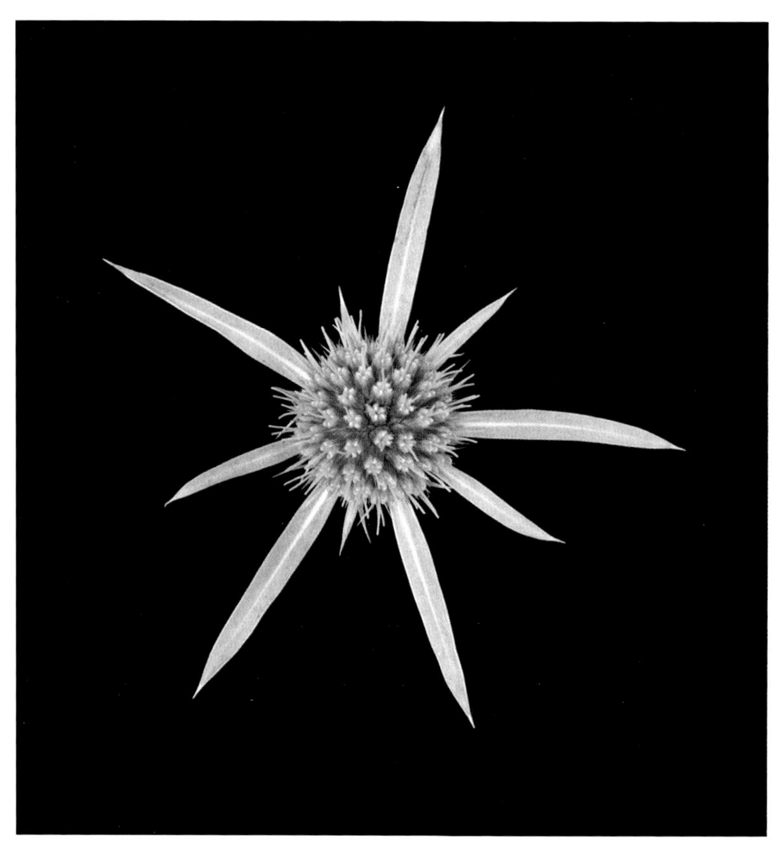

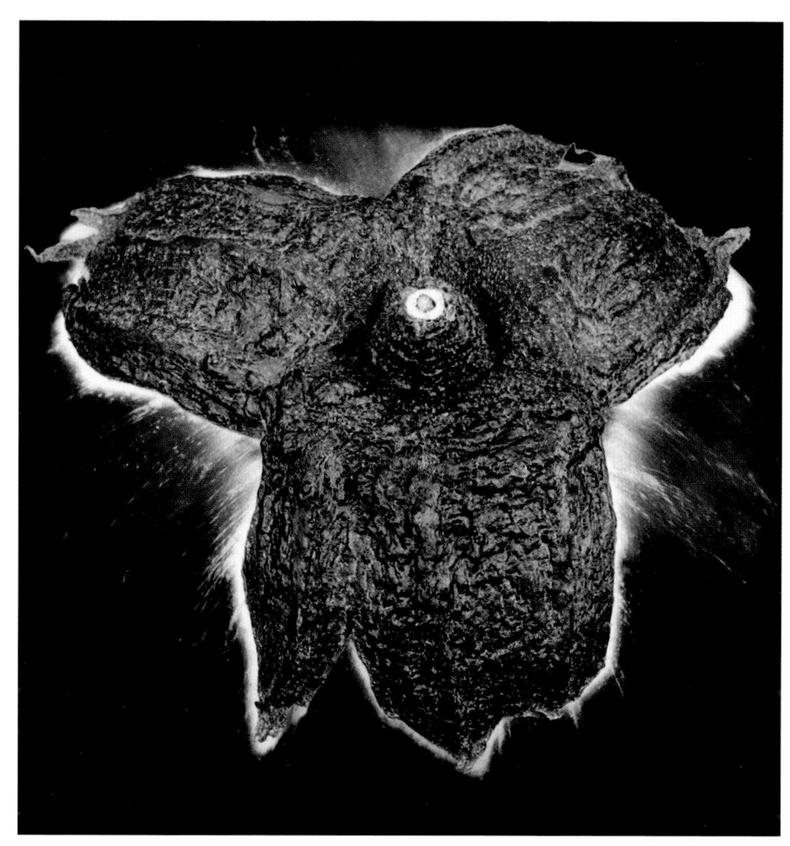

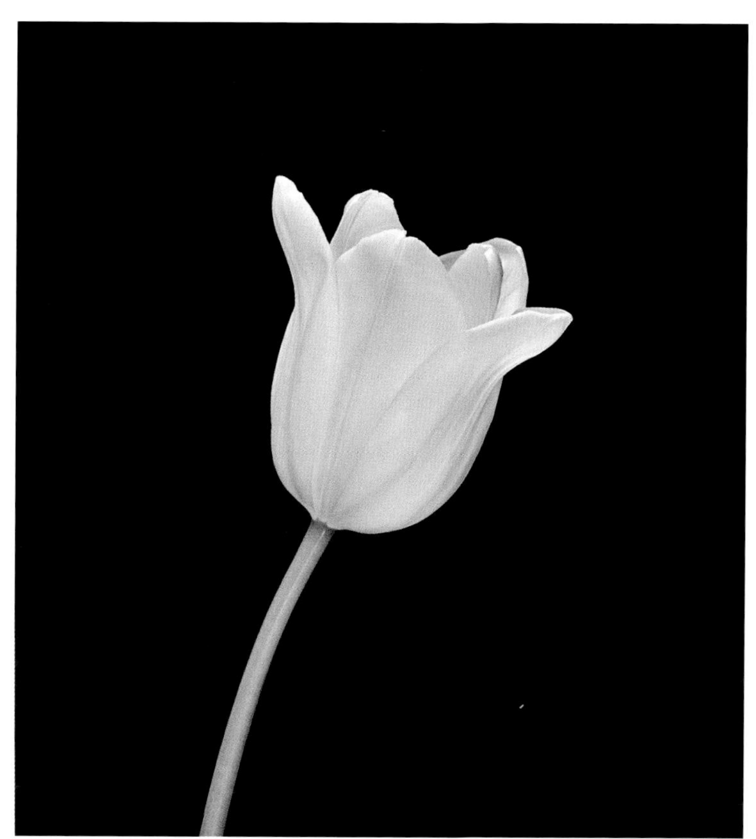

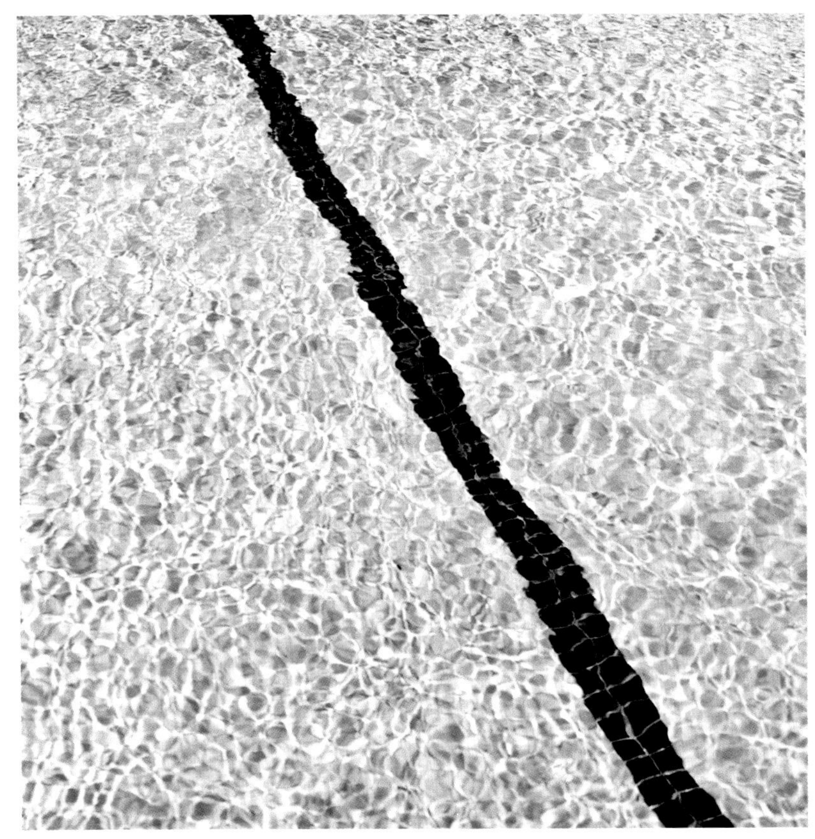

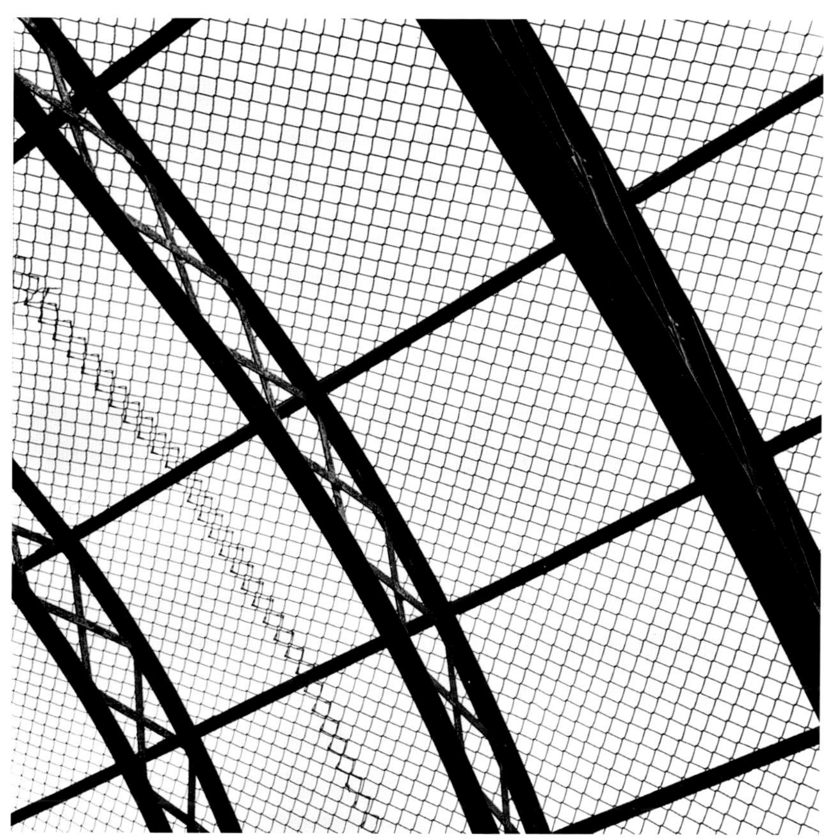

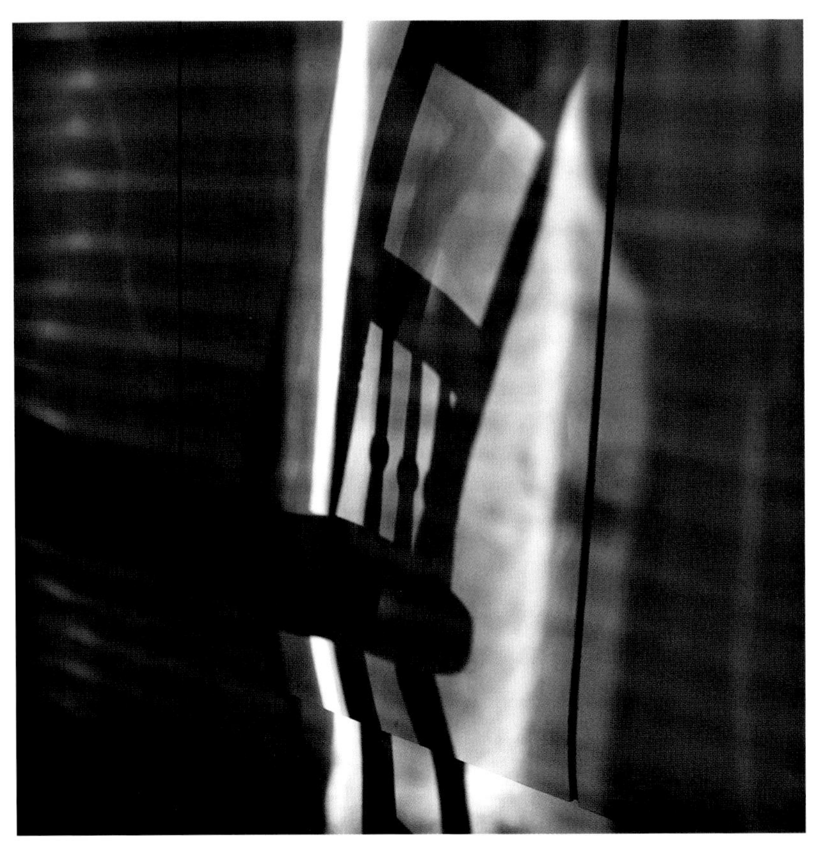

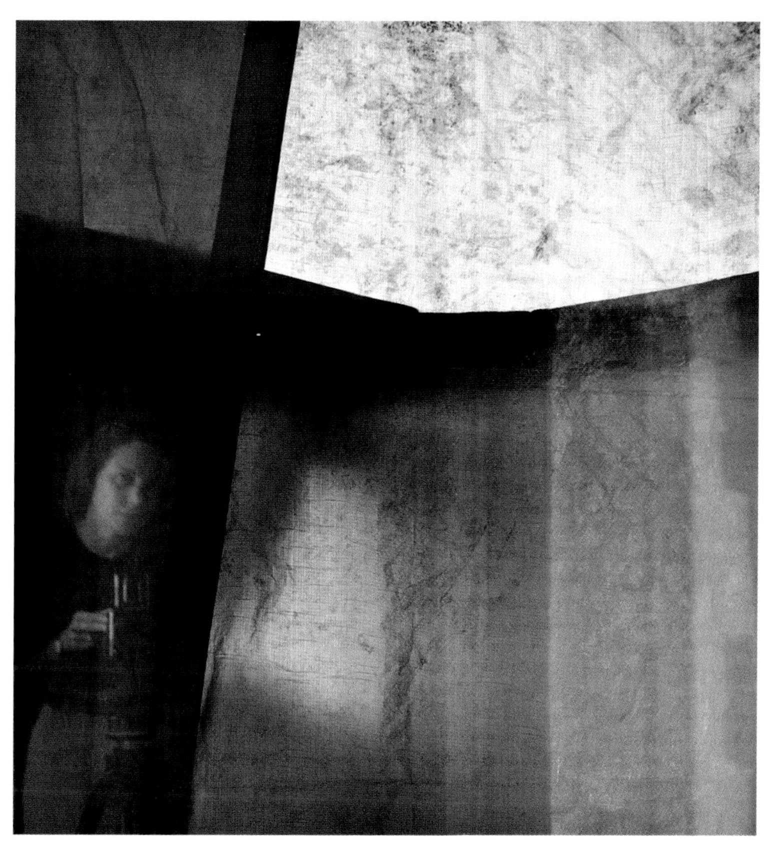

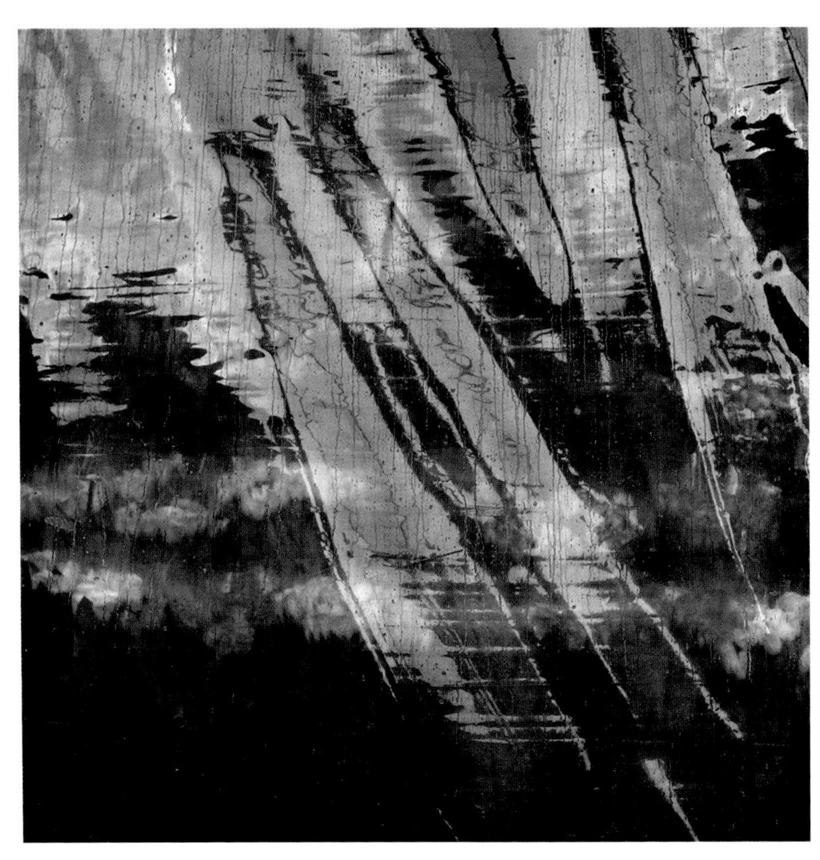

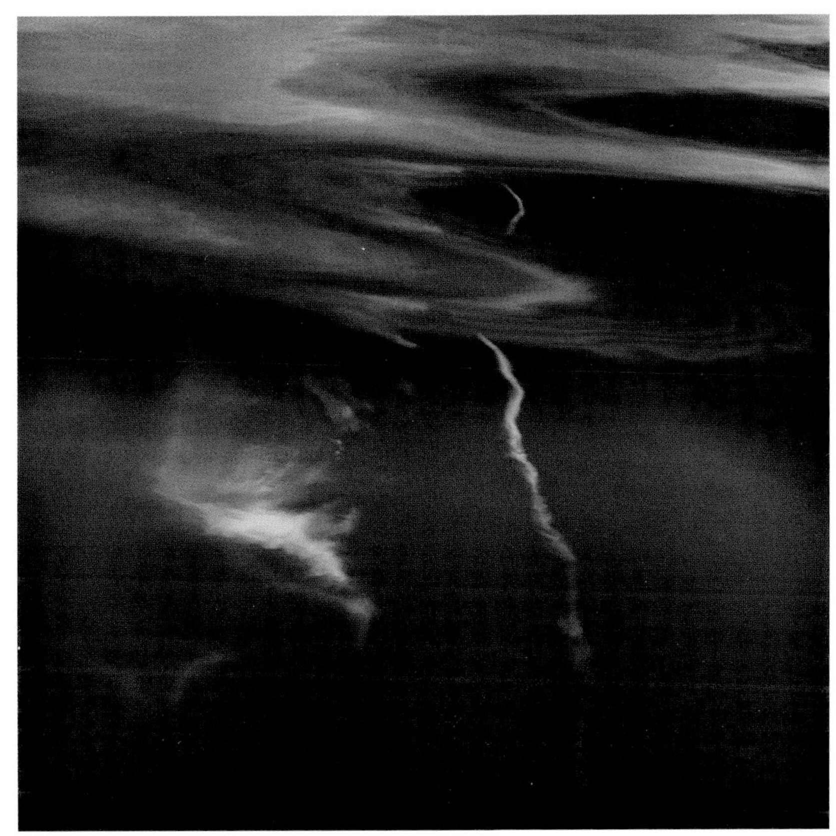

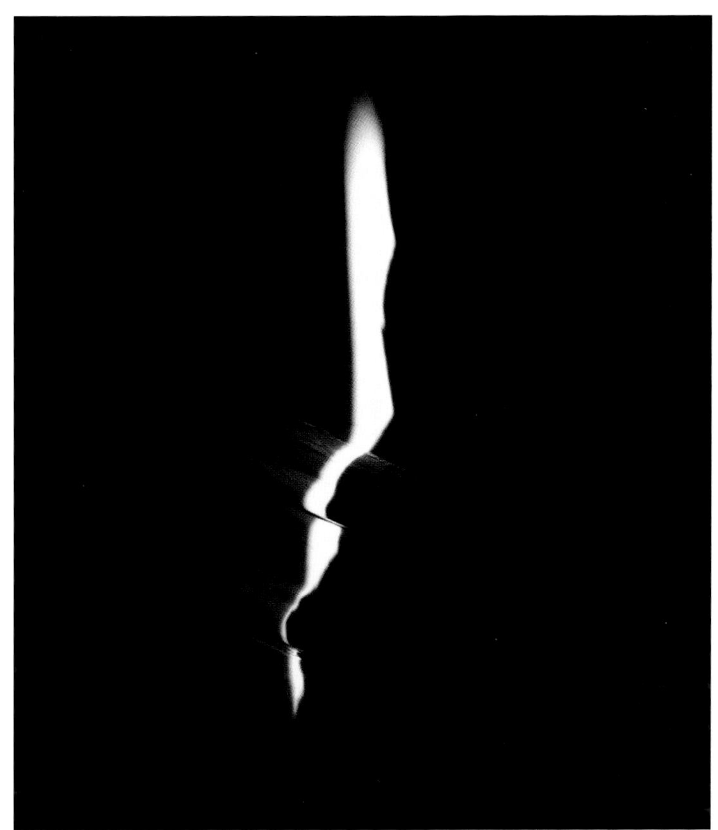

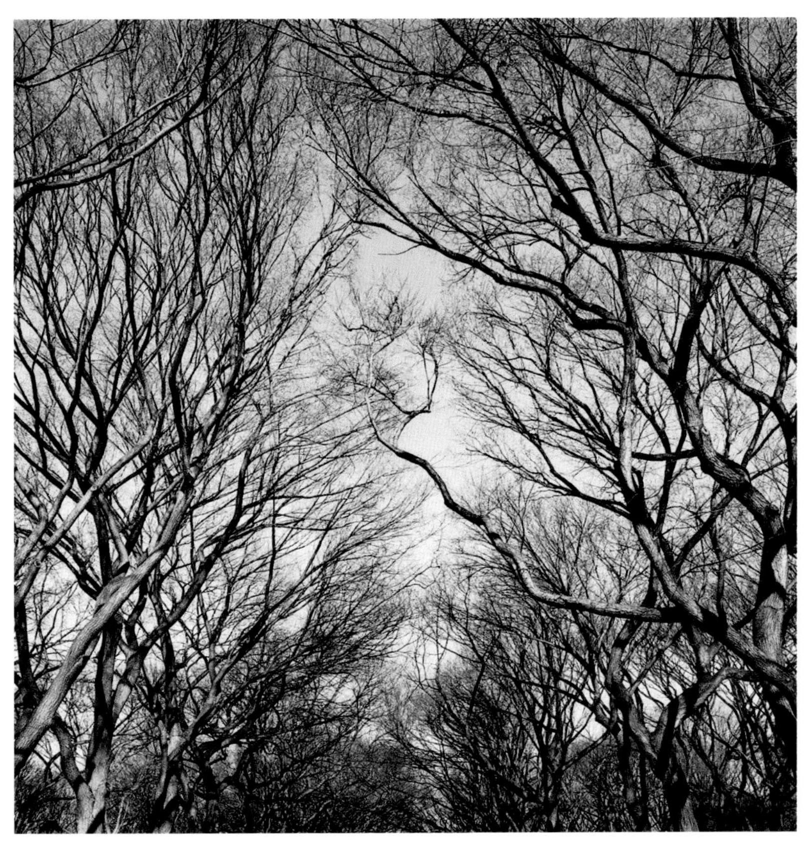

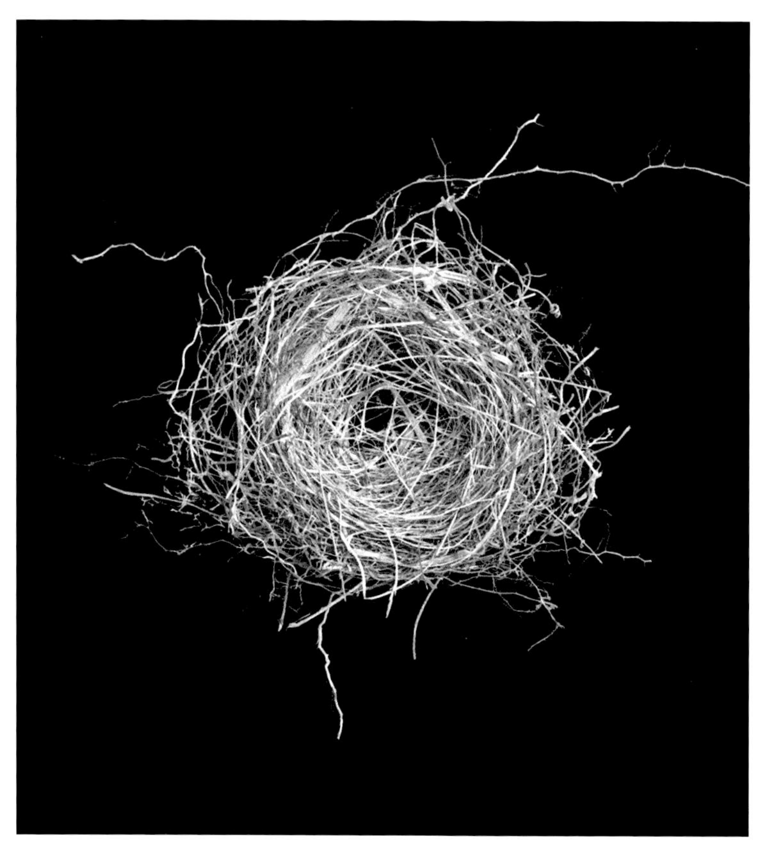

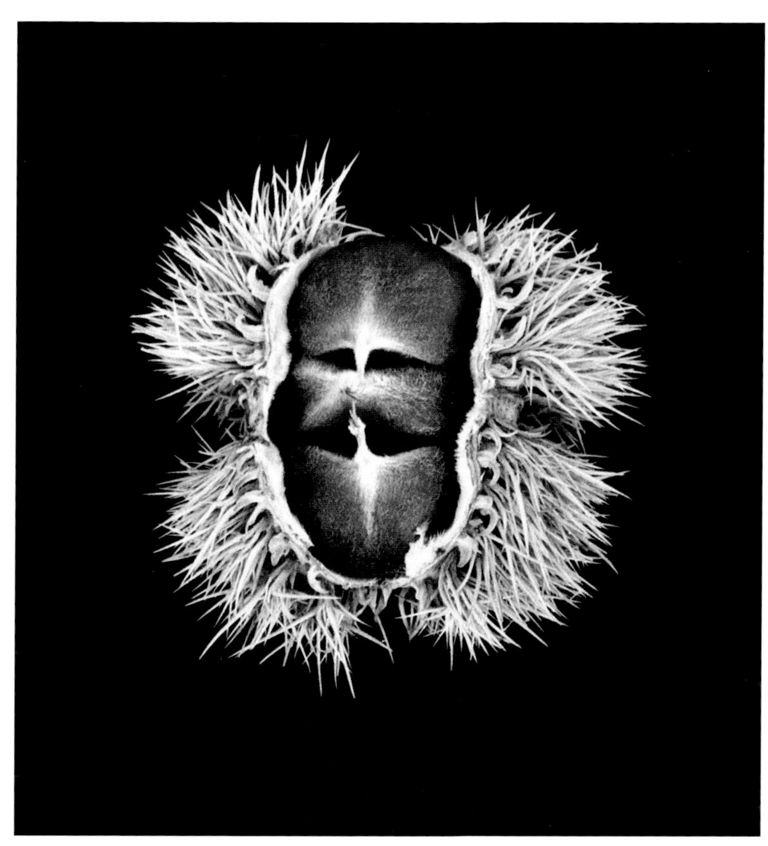

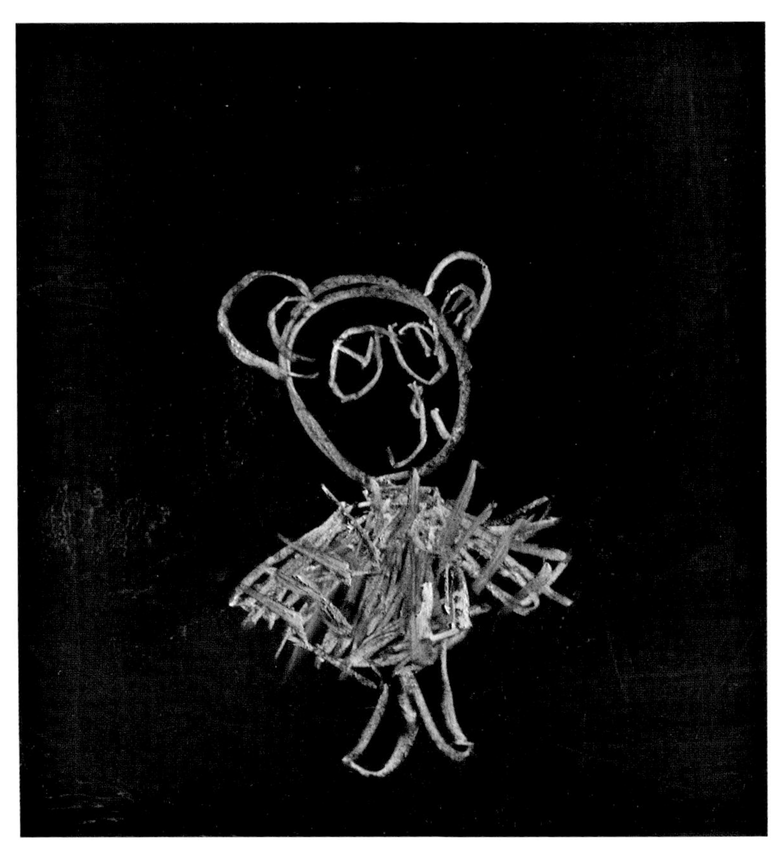

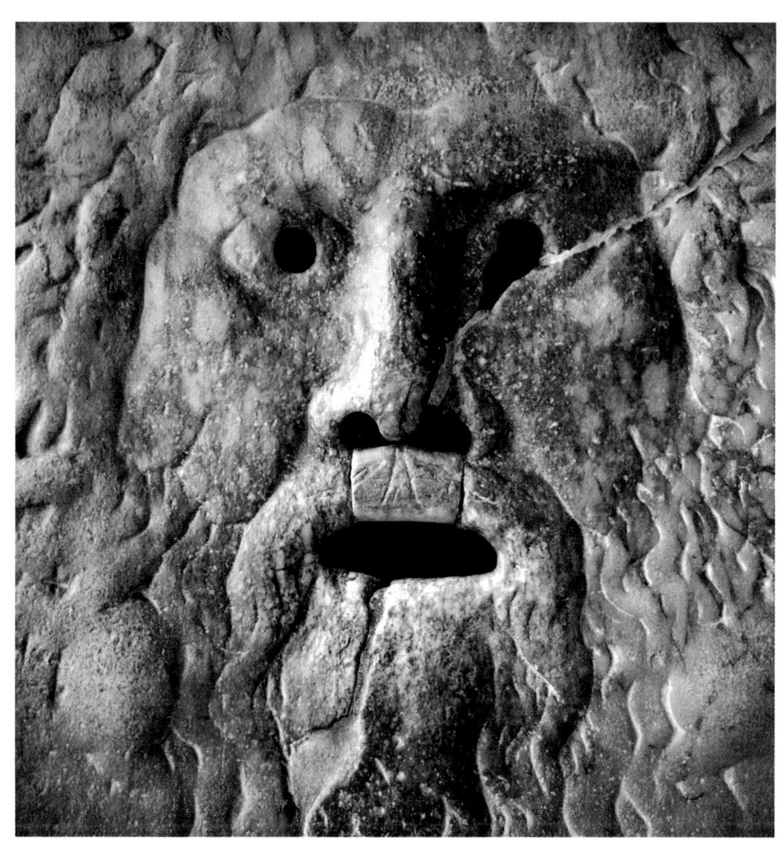

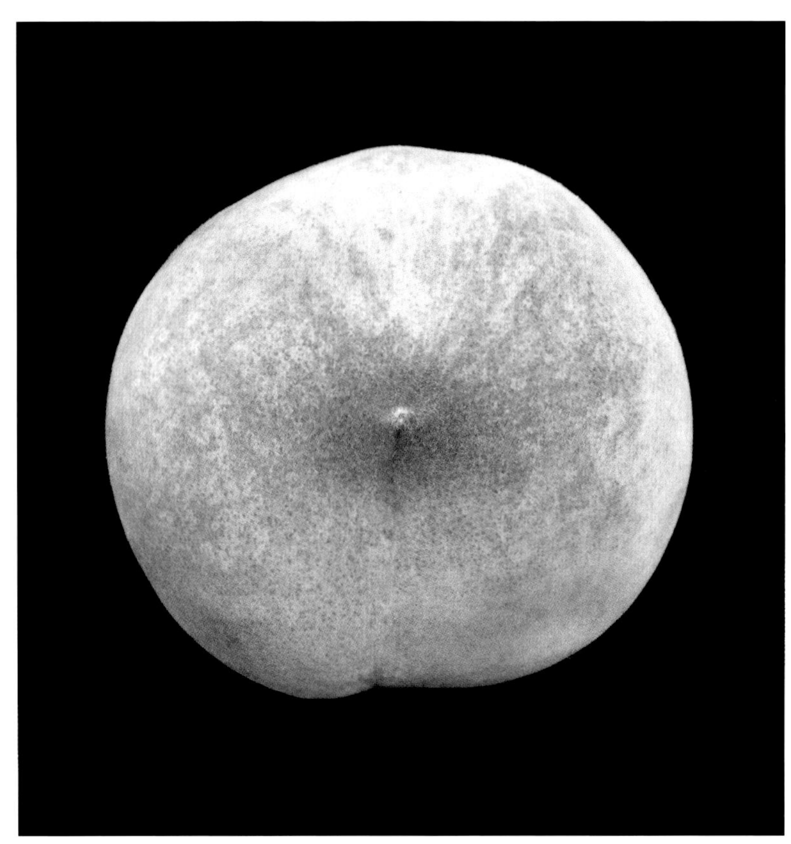

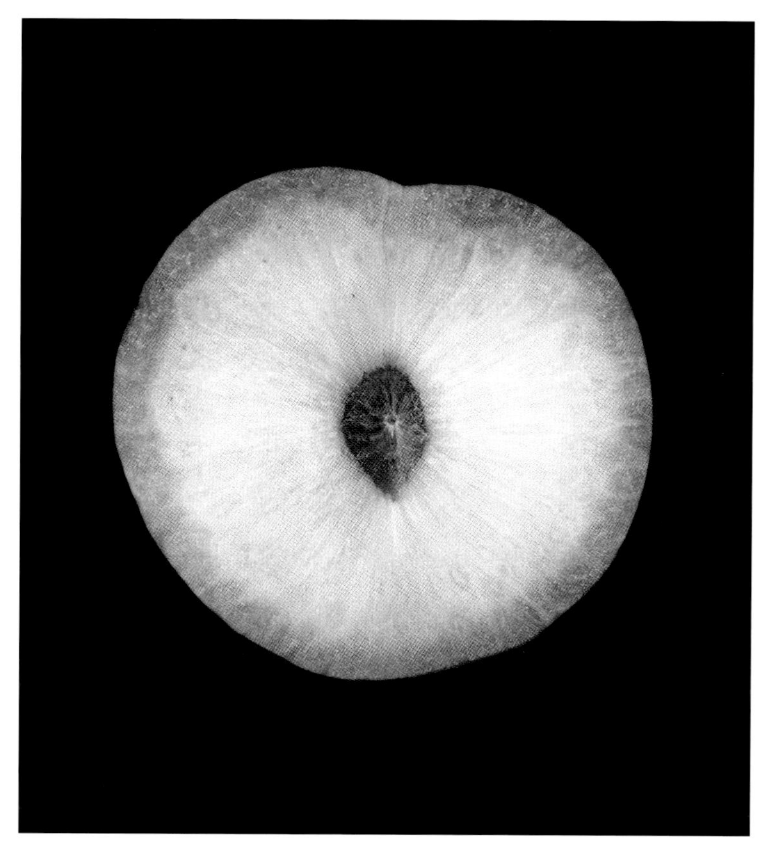

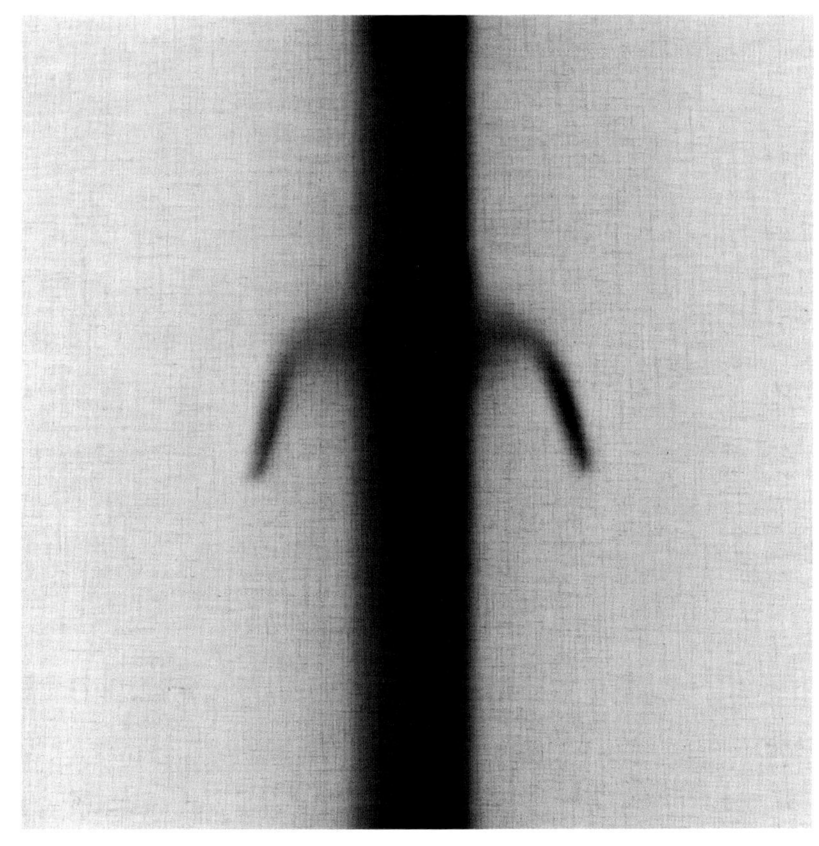

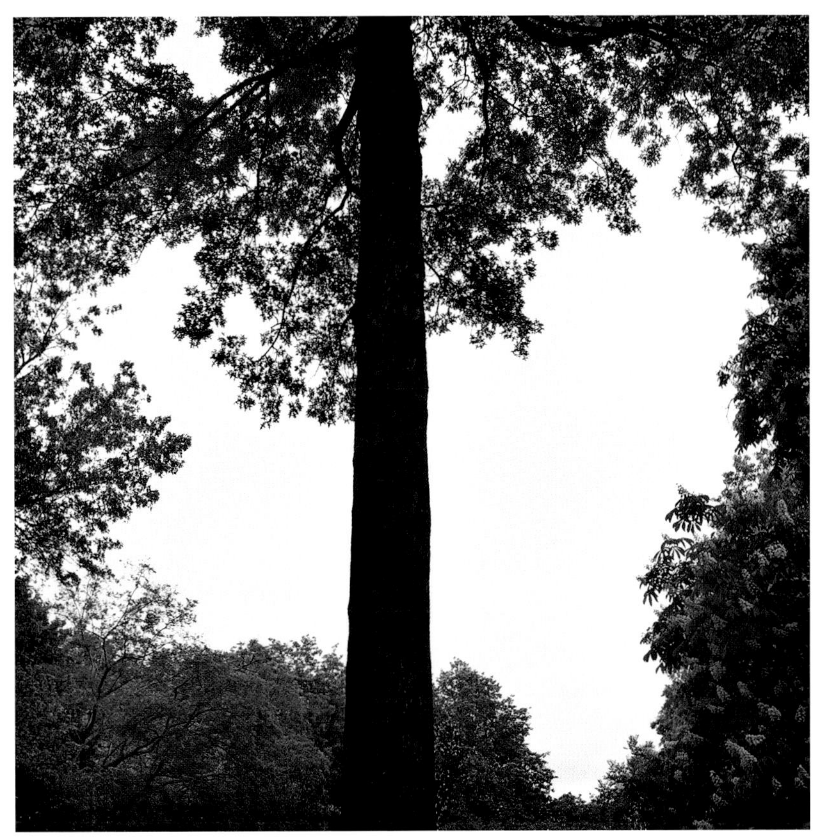

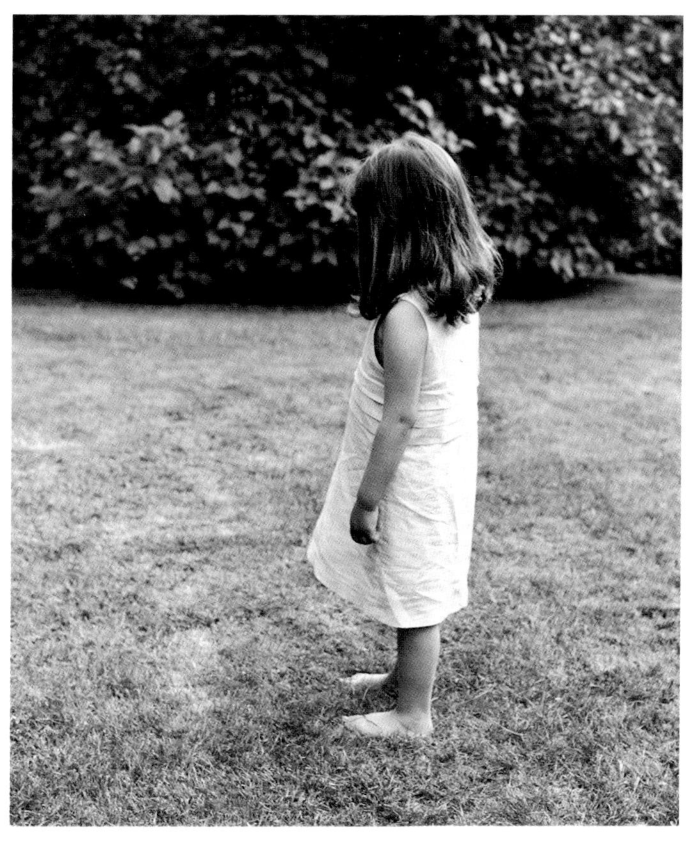

CAPTIONS TO THE IMAGES

2 *Barbara's Pears*
West Tisbury, Massachusetts
10 October 1999, 10:30 a.m.

6 *Clouds and Tree*
West Tisbury, Massachusetts
8 August 1999, 5:00 p.m.

17 *Egg*
New York City
23 September 1999, 5:10 p.m.

19 *Sweet Feet*
Kona Village, Hawaii
5 January 1999, 7:30 a.m.

21 *Mountain*
Glion, Switzerland
19 June 1999, 9:00 p.m.

22 *Oak Leaf*
New York City
31 October 2000, 9:40 a.m.

23 *Shadow of My Hand*
New York City
8 October 1999, 6:05 p.m.

24 *Anthurium Crystallinum*
New York City
11 January 2001, 4:25 p.m.

25 *Cabbage*
New York City
6 September 2000, 4:55 p.m.

26 *Lamp in Light*
New York City
3 January 2000, 7:40 a.m.

27 *Bosc Pear*
New York City
7 December 2000, 3:00 p.m.

28 *Yo-yos*
Basel, Switzerland
16 June 1999, 11:55 a.m.

29 *Brown Beech Mushrooms*
New York City
1 May 2000, 5:25 p.m.

30 *Pool Steps Under Water*
Anguilla, West Indies
29 March 2006, 3:50 p.m.

31 *Three Triangles*
St. Moritz, Switzerland
25 December 2006, 3:10 p.m.

32 *Platane Tree Bark*
Gassin, France
2 July 2000, 8:30 a.m.

33 *Construction Tarp*
New York City
3 October 1999, 11:45 a.m.

35 *Thistle*
West Tisbury, Massachusetts
29 July 2000, 11:25 a.m.

37 *Emily and Caterpillar*
Saint-Barthélemy, West Indies
22 March 2000, 3:30 p.m.

38 *Kitty Cat*
New York City
25 May 1999, 5:50 p.m.

39 *Ginger*
New York City
1 February 2000, 2:10 p.m.

40 *Pussy Willows*
New York City
24 February 1999, 5:15 p.m.

41 *Savine's Dress*
New York City
23 January 1999, 4:30 p.m.

43 *Pancakes*
New York City
28 March 1999, 2:30 p.m.

45 *Beach Chairs*
Kona Village, Hawaii
4 January 1999, 6:30 p.m.

46 *Doorknob*
New York City
20 January 1999, 4:15 p.m.

Shade Cord
New York City
1 May 1999, 4:35 p.m.

47 *Door Jamb*
New York City
22 January 2001, 3:20 p.m.

Shade, Cord and Shadows
New York City
26 November 1999, 3:40 p.m.

48 *Light on Road*
Saint-Barthélemy, West Indies
3 January 2001, 7:40 a.m.

49 *Shadow*
Saint-Barthélemy, West Indies
4 January 2001, 5:00 p.m.

50 *Oak Tree*
Santa Barbara, California
22 January 2000, 4:50 p.m.

51 *Mom and I Holding Hands*
New York City
25 August 2004, 4:15 p.m.

53 *Treetops and Clouds*
New York City
4 March 1999, 11:00 a.m.

54 *Orchid Plant*
New York City
9 February 2000, 4:00 p.m.

55 *Chilmark Oak*
Chilmark, Massachusetts
13 March 1999, 10:30 a.m.

56 *Hydrangea*
New York City
6 January 1999, 5:00 p.m.

57 *Wasp Nest*
North Bennington, Vermont
16 September 2006, 2:20 p.m.

59 *Three Birch Trees*
Kent, Connecticut
19 February 2006, 8:25 a.m.

61 *Blind Chicken*
Kent, Connecticut
19 February 1999, 11:00 a.m.

62 *Veronica*
New York City
25 November 2000, 9:25 a.m.

63 *Mushroom*
Berkeley, California
25 March 2001, 12:20 p.m.

64 *Cubanelle Pepper*
New York City
11 April 2000, 4:00 p.m.

65 *Emily's Foot*
Glion, Switzerland
18 June 1999, 8:05 p.m.

67 *Horizon*
Bermuda
26 April 2000, 6:00 p.m.

68 *Clouds, Lambert's Cove*
West Tisbury, Massachusetts
14 July 1999, 4:05 p.m.

69 *Hazelnuts*
New York City
13 May 1999, 4:40 p.m.

70 *Sand*
Chilmark, Massachusetts
13 July 2001, 1:20 p.m.

71 *Rhine River*
Basel, Switzerland
13 June 2001, 9:45 a.m.

73 *Flying Bird*
West Tisbury, Massachusetts
23 August 1999, 2:30 p.m.

74 *Clouds*
New York City
29 September 2001, 12:15 p.m.

75 *Light*
Kona Village, Hawaii
1 January 1999, 7:50 a.m.

76 *Light Line*
Madrid, Spain
19 June 2001, 7:05 p.m.

Light in Form of Flag
Antigua, West Indies
16 February 2001, 3:20 p.m.

77 *Arrow of Light*
New York City
10 September 2005, 3:33 p.m.

Light Bands
New York City
22 August 2004, 7:00 p.m.

79 *Allen's Hat*
North Bennington, Vermont
31 May 1999, 10:20 a.m.

80 *Oyster*
New York City
10 October 2001, 2:10 p.m.

81 *Jellyfish*
New York City
26 November 2001, 2:25 p.m.

82 *Bale of Hay*
West Tisbury, Massachusetts
27 July 2000, 5:50 p.m.

83 *Sourdough Boule*
New York City
8 February 2000, 2:25 p.m.

84 *Chayote*
New York City
17 April 2000, 3:20 p.m.

85 *Melon*
New York City
31 March 2000, 2:00 p.m.

86 *Kiwi*
Chilmark, Massachusetts
2 August 2002, 5:25 p.m.

Vase
New York City
1 February 2002, 3:25 p.m.

87 *Stonemason's Bucket*
Chilmark, Massachusetts
31 July 2000, 6:30 p.m.

Pantheon
Rome, Italy
10 June 1999, 5:15 p.m.

89 *Apple*
New York City
3 December 2000, 4:05 p.m.

91 *Child's Torso*
New York City
12 March 2000, 3:50 p.m.

92 *Astilboides*
North Bennington, Vermont
29 May 1999, 7:45 p.m.

93 *Baby's Dress*
New York City
10 September 1999, 12:30 p.m.

94 *Cherry Tree in Blossom*
New York City
14 April 1999, 2:00 p.m.

95 *Starfish*
Paris, France
19 June 2000, 10:40 a.m.

96 *Thistle Flower*
Chilmark, Massachusetts
22 June 2002, 2:20 p.m.

97 *Eggplant*
New York City
20 May 2000, 11:15 a.m.

99 *White Tulip*
New York City
7 February 2000, 1:45 p.m.

100 *Pool*
Carmel, California
22 May 1999, 10:30 a.m.

101 *Roof, 92nd Street Y*
New York City
21 April 1999, 10:15 a.m.

102 *Chair Shadow*
New York City
31 May 2001, 7:10 p.m.

103 *Self-Portrait*
New York City
28 September 1999, 11:50 a.m.

104 *Flowers Behind Plastic*
New York City
27 January 2001, 9:15 a.m.

105 *Water Reflection*
Menemsha, Massachusetts
31 August 1999, 6:50 p.m.

107 *Sliver of Light*
New York City
22 August 2004, 6:50 p.m.

109 *Central Park Trees*
New York City
17 January 1999, 12:00 p.m.

110 *Bird's Nest*
Chilmark, Massachusetts
28 July 2001, 2:40 p.m.

111 *Chestnut*
New York City
31 October 2001, 2:40 p.m.

112 *Chalk Bear*
New York City
10 November 2001, 8:30 a.m.

113 *Bocca Della Verita*
Rome, Italy
11 June 1999, 12:00 p.m.

114 *White Peach*
Basel, Switzerland
16 June 2001, 6:10 p.m.

115 *Plum*
Chilmark, Massachusetts
3 September 2001, 11:10 a.m.

117 *Shaded Window Handles*
New York City
1 May 1999, 4:30 p.m.

119 *Tree Trunk in Sky*
New York City
11 May 2000, 9:50 a.m.

121 *Emily*
Claire Fontaine, France
26 June 1999, 8:30 p.m.

127 *Rusty and His Ball*
Chilmark, Massachusetts
3 July 2006, 4:10 p.m.

128 *Muddy Road*
West Tisbury, Massachusetts
14 August 2000, 12:20 p.m.

Reproductions made from the photographer's original silver gelatin prints.

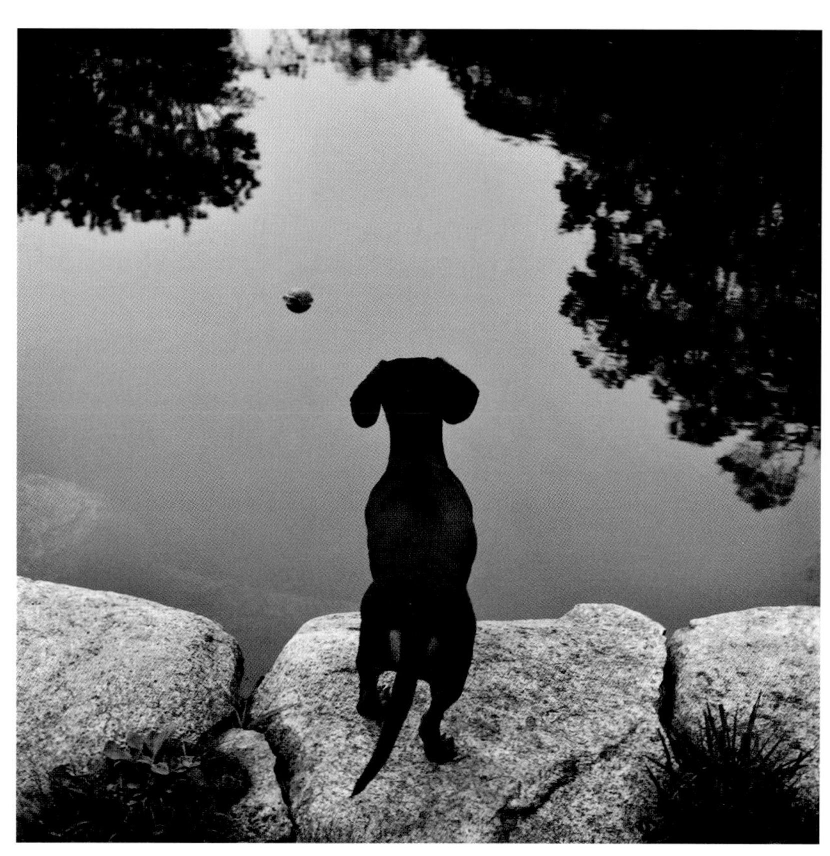

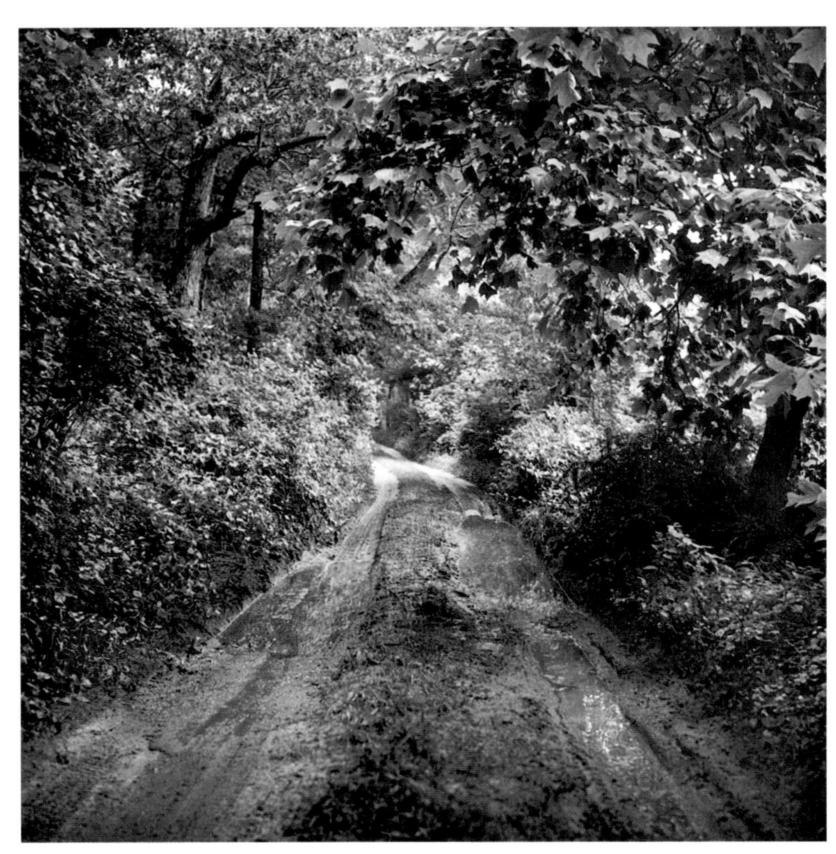